Adapted

By
Josh Barry

Josh Barry

Published: August 2018 by FCM Publishing
FCM Publishing

ISBN: 9781999652661
Paperback Edition

This book is a memoir, reflecting the author's present recollections of experiences over time. Some names and characteristics have been changed, some events have been compressed, and some dialogue has been recreated. Memory can be a fickle thing, so the Author trusts that any minor errors in times, dates and details of particular events will be understood.

Some names and identifying details have been changed to protect the privacy of individuals.

Cover Image by Michael Butters Photography
Cover design by Luke Buxton

Contents

Dedication

This book is dedicated to the life and memory of Joy Trueman: a loving mother, doting grandmother and loyal friend. We miss you every day.

Acknowledgements

So here we go, the bit where I thank everyone… I suppose it's a bit like a written down Oscar's speech. As you're about to discover, my life is all about teamwork and the collaboration of brain and brawn. If I was to list everyone who had a contributing factor in me writing this book, I would be here until next Christmas. Suffice to say, these are the abridged acknowledgements and if I have missed anyone out, blame the typist!

Firstly, my special thanks goes to the many personal assistants who have effortlessly and patiently scribed all of my utterances, no matter how random they have been (if they've been too random I've resorted to typing them out on my iPad!). To my family and friends; without them, this book would not even be in existence… I guess I wouldn't either! Additionally, I would like to express my gratitude to the writer and broadcaster John Hannam for the spectacular foreword which you're about to read, all of it is absolutely true! More generally, thank you to everyone who is mentioned in the book, for good or for bad, you gave me something to write about!

An extended gratitude goes to those many people who assisted with my development research and so kindly gave of their time. But mainly a humongous thank you to everyone who has helped me with everything I have accomplished over the years. Most importantly, Mum, Dad, Lauren and Soph for your devoted and selfless support, shaping me into the man I am and for helping me to realise my potential. Then there's Alice, Beryl and Di for your hard work and patience, not forgetting Penny and Maretta for helping to build the foundations of my academia. Moving on from school to university, a big thank you has to go to Ann Beech, John Walker, Joe Frodsham, Tom Rehaag, Ian Thompson, Steve Barton, Jackie Kay, Jill Good, Debbie Whatton, Irene Hewitt, Hayley Barrington and Ruth Johnston for your assistance and patience whilst at university, you made the perfect team. In addition, while on the subject of university, I owe a massive debt of gratitude to Jan Weddup, John Foster, Phil Mathews and Jo Tyler for their encouragement and constant influence throughout and beyond my university experience.

A big thanks to Taryn Johnston and all at FCM Publishing for believing in the project and specifically for Taryn's patience during several painstaking drafts!

Finally to the many quality carers I have had the pleasure to work with over the years, so many that I couldn't list you all, but you know who you are and you know how you have changed my life. Thank you so much to each and every one of you!

Foreword

I have been a devoted follower of the British show-business scene since the moment I first saw a real variety show at the Theatre Royal, Portsmouth, back in the early '50s. Sadly, these marvellous shows are now virtually extinct. I was privileged to see the stars of the times, like Michael Bentine, Brian Reece (PC 49), Frankie Vaughan, Jon Pertwee and Tony Brent. My memories include autographs I waited for at the stage door.

These memories have also been enhanced in the past 18 months due to meeting Josh Barry. Despite being so young, he has an incredible knowledge of the halcyon days of artists and their agents. Some real top pros have shared my enthusiasm for his devotion to and great love for, the good old days of the theatre industry.

Josh has a remarkable story and, thankfully, he survived his difficult birth. This seemed unlikely at one time. He's always been a fighter and we love him for it. People from all walks of life marvel at his achievements and his real zest for life. I, personally, love his sense of humour - and he can certainly give as good as he gets. It is a real honour to write this foreword for Josh and I know you will be touched by his amazing story. He has always had dreams and already he has achieved many of them.

I only have one complaint with young Mr Barry. I have visited him on numerous occasions and have yet to find any milk in his house. I look forward to one day having coffee with milk and a little less Ribena and orange squash. In my life I have been lucky enough to have met thousands of famous people but none have moved me more than Josh Barry.

John Hannam
Showbiz writer and broadcaster.

I

Introduction

So, you have spent your well-earned money on what you hope will be a great read. Or, had they just run out books about the latest reality star and you thought you would give this a go? Irrespective of how you got here, thank you for putting a bit of me into your life (unless you're like me and you buy books that stay on your bookshelf for years and years, collecting dust). In that case you won't have read this yet so it doesn't matter. But, if you are reading, well I hope you won't be disappointed… Although if you are, it could make a lovely second-hand Christmas present for a distant relative or something to put in the British Heart Foundation charity bag. Assuming that you're feeling brave, I invite you on the trip of a lifetime. My lifetime.

You may already have many preconceived ideas of what this book could be about, and you're not alone. When I started writing it, I thought I had a very clear vision of what I wanted to say and the purpose of the book. But after writing it, I'm not sure my motives are still relevant. I have changed my opinions on how I see myself and my disability as a result of the way I've reflected on my experiences, achievements and regrets. So, you might actually take away something completely different from my original intention. As it's evolved, my purposes for writing it have expanded to encapsulate different areas of my life, so I hope it provides something for everyone.

Perhaps it's an uplifting story of how a disabled man overcame obstacles against all the odds to become a bastion of disability in a mainstream world? Or even a self-obsessed writer who demands the world to know how hard his journey is as a result of his Cerebral Palsy? Then again it could be a self-help book for other CP sufferers to take some solace from, and be inspired by, the way I have lived my life. Honestly, what a load of crap! I'm hardly a saint, I'm no disabled role model. Christ, if you saw me pissed up in my hometown on a Friday night, I think you'd agree! Indeed it could be argued that my whole life has been about changing people's perception of disability and constantly adapting everyday concepts to attempt to fit into the mainstream. I love to make people laugh and leave an indelible impression on someone, which I hope you get from reading this book. When I think about it, my whole life has been about making people aware that between the wheels, dribble and spasms, there's actually a light on (somewhere!). This has been helped by the things I've done, places I've been and the people I've met. So, here's my opportunity to tell you a little about them and how they have each helped me to achieve my hopes, dreams and aspirations.

I feel I should begin with the basics. Allow me to introduce myself; my name is Josh Barry, I was born and grew up on the Isle of Wight and at the time of writing, in 2018, I am thirty years old. What do you need to know about me? I tell terrible jokes, I loved Cilla Black, my favourite drink is spiced rum and coke with half a lime and... Oh yeah... I suffer from Athetoid Cerebral Palsy following complications with my birth. The Cerebral Palsy bit I thought I'd put last as a little twist, a bit like when you watch an episode of Midsummer Murders and you're convinced it's the wife who committed mass homicide but it turns out to be the cuddly old housekeeper!

Now for the scientific bit… Athetoid Cerebral Palsy means messages from my brain to my whole body are a little jumbled. This results in me having a lot of involuntary movement and my speech is difficult to understand to the untrained ear. I lack dexterity in order to carry out menial physical tasks. I can't balance or weight bear unaided and therefore use a wheelchair to get around and employ a team of "people" to facilitate my life in the way I wish to live it. I always find it very difficult to categorise these people. Are they "carers" or "helpers" or "Personal Assistants" or does it matter? As you would expect, this is much more complicated than it sounds for reasons which will be discussed in depth later. I am a masters graduate of Bournemouth University where I undertook an arts degree in 'Scriptwriting for Film and Television' followed by an MA in 'Writing for the Media'. I'm a freelance writer who literally writes with my nose, no seriously, on an iPad!

Throughout my life, I have been very conscious of the fact that people remain fascinated by the way disabled people function within the rules of mainstream life and specifically the way I go about living mine. I often forget that I am indeed in this minority and have grown acclimatised to the fact that almost everyone close to me regards me as a fully functioning and able person. It is only when I am in public places and become the subject of attention by staring toddlers or the glare of a fascinated onlooker that I am reminded I am different to the average Joe. So by putting my life on paper the reader may get a little insight into what it's like having a physical disability in a mainstream world.

In my thirty years on this earth I haven't done that much out of the ordinary. I haven't gone to the moon, I haven't been the first black president of America, and I haven't even won the World Cup. Compared to this, my life will seem a little boring. For God's sake, I watch EastEnders every night and I'm not keen on sunshine, how dull do you want me to get?! Yet, what I have done is attempted to live a mainstream life whilst having to understand and challenge my limitations as a disabled man. Some people say that my life isn't “ordinary” at all; you could say I have lived an ‘adapted’ life…

II

With a Little Help from my Friends

Now personally, I prefer Joe Cocker's version better than The Beatles (something for the more mature reader) but you'll come to understand that I never do anything expected.

Here we go... and we're off and running! There's certain information you should know in order to understand the book. Having Cerebral Palsy, I've needed assistance with pretty much everything I've done; be it someone attempting to run me around a field after a football (it looked more like Bambi on Ice!) or scribing my work. My whole life has been about teamwork and the combination of brain and brawn to help me achieve my potential.

In a recent article about me, written to promote a radio documentary project, for some reason they felt that they had to include "a special mention to Josh's carers". I didn't get it. Whilst no, I couldn't have attended the interview without help or indeed written the documentary, I didn't feel it was the time or place for a carer mention. Surely the comparison is of the transcriber being acknowledged for someone who can't type… Obviously there are a lot of people who are responsible for making me the man I am and I can't wait to tell you a little about them, but I do feel that there is definitely a time and a place for acknowledging assistance and sometimes it's just not appropriate.

On occasions this feeling manifests itself into thoughts about my own manhood and what it is to be a man. I will admit to feeling stripped of that masculinity from time to time, through not being able to carry out the easiest of meaningless tasks. This is sometimes exacerbated by my decision to employ helpers who are around my age or younger, as I can see how much they thrive on their own masculinity and I sometimes feel like I have none. However, from a positive aspect it means that I am never without a mate to enjoy experiences with and to echo my life. I still don't know how to describe this feeling of masculinity or lack of. Is it a problem with my masculinity or a realisation that no matter how hard I try, I'll never be physically independent?

From unscrewing a stiff jar to carrying heavy objects from place to place (I'll never be a barman!), I am physically incapable and where I could just surmise that it is a rather small part of everyday life, it remains the only thing that irritates me about my disability. This may be a revelation to you, as if you saw me in the street you would think that I have nothing going on 'upstairs', but I don't care about that. It's the fact of knowing that no matter how hard I try I will never be a stereotypical man who can be relied upon to do "man-things" (sorry this has turned into one of those housewife books from the 1950's).

To combat this, I've always tried to join in with "normal" fun. My Mum often recalls taking me to rugby practice at the age of nine and running me around the pitch, until one of the bigger boys wanted to tackle me. Mum was and still is ever-loving and would do anything for me but that was where she drew the line and I don't blame her! I think you'll agree that sometimes I do take the whole "manhood" thing to the absolute extreme, nothing says "grrr" like a good old game of rugby. Yet irrespective of the sport or game, I was where I wanted to be; just a normal guy with his mates. This acceptance is what I've been striving for my whole life and whilst it might no longer be on a rugby pitch my desire for this social freedom remains the same.

Now, I'm conscious not to sound like the voiceover from The X-Factor but to introduce major figures in this story, I've got the urge to write their names in capitals with bold and underlined text. Alice Turner and Beryl Copeland had such a positive effect on my childhood, that if they had ever appeared on my version of the Michael Parkinson Show, they most certainly would have been top of the bill. Alice and Beryl were introduced to the whole Barry family when I was just a week old. Mum and Dad were still extremely frightened as to what the future held for me and my whole family. Delicately and lovingly, Alice and Beryl advised and supported families coping with a new disabled member. One Thursday each month, Alice and Beryl ran a group called Toy Library which provided an opportunity for these families to come together in an informal setting so that they wouldn't feel judged or inspected. It was here that Alice recognised I was suffering from extreme attachment issues as a result of only being handled by my Mum, Dad and Gran.

Alice made it her mission to improve this situation and each Thursday afternoon she and Beryl would come to our house and arrange excursions in order to make me more independent. At first these were tiny little steps, like pushing me up the road and back again but they slowly evolved into more elaborate outings and more often than not my twin sister, Sophie came along for the ride. Whether it was afternoon tea at a posh cafe, putting my hands in rag worm or climbing on the roof of Alice's house, whatever we did with Alice and Beryl was always loaded with incredible amounts of fun, even if I'll never know how I actually got up on that roof!

Luckily, they both became permanent fixtures in my life and were always on hand to help me celebrate my many successes. Twenty years after their retirement, our families remained close and stayed on top of each other's news and gossip. Yet tragedy struck in 2016 when Alice suffered a debilitating stroke and tragically passed away. This affected me in ways I thought it wouldn't. She was one of the first people to believe that I could lead a normal life and always pushed me to tackle bigger and better things. It meant so much to have her tell me she was proud of me. Her encouragement and support over the years was invaluable and I just hope that she knew how special she was.

Alice and Beryl laid the foundations for me to obtain independence away from my family which was so important to the development of my life. When I was nine-years-old, I needed more freedom and so my parents approached a fifteen-year-old school boy, who was known to the family through his sister, to see if he could help provide this. It was decided that he should be taken on for two hours a week on a Tuesday. Unbeknown to all, this fifteen year old, Calum Robertson, would become my unofficial big brother, doing all the things that a big brother should do. I was nine and started to look at the world around me in a different way. I wanted to know about the birds and the bees (quite literally). I never had a big brother or someone who could show me what it was like to be a man and Calum provided that. Even now, almost a quarter of a century later, whenever I'm in need of advice or support, Calum remains at the top of my call register. He also remained a significant figure within my care team for the best part of fifteen years and gradually was able to cultivate his technique of working with me which I feel has never been surpassed.

You could say it was like a very unusual "Match made in Heaven" (not that Calum would ever put my name and marriage in the same sentence… even the thought of it would kill him!) He knew my needs so well and knew how to cater for them. So, when another carer who didn't fit the bill came into the mix, it was frustrating for Calum to see. Having someone older and (dare I say it) wiser than me was a bonus for my friends as it meant their parents were a lot more lenient on what they did because there was apparently an adult present. It still makes me laugh referring to Calum as a wise adult, there is nothing boringly mature about him at all. But I also realise this advantage for my friends was something that I could have been used for. If I was gonna integrate myself within a group of able-bodied people, I wanted them to want me there for who I was, not for the benefit I could bring them and I was lucky enough that my friends were better than that.

It is only with hindsight that I realise how difficult this was for Calum to gauge and how pivotal this became to my social interaction. My friends soon realised that Calum was not there to be a make shift child minder, he was just there to put me on the same level as everyone else. If that meant running me around the Rec whilst playing manhunt or roller-skating with me, then that was what he did.

Calum wasn't the only poor unfortunate youth who agreed to take the occasionally prestigious title of my "carer". I needed someone to compliment Calum's "Jack the Lad" image. Someone intelligent, responsible and caring, but you don't always get what you want! Steve was nineteen-years-old when I met him at a barn dance (I'll explain later, it's a long story).

He was able to make the perfect carer for almost fifteen years and his mature approach gave me another facet to my life. It was with Steve that I realised my great love of researching the history of entertainment when I was given the Radio Times Encyclopaedia of British Comedy. Steve and I would spend hours upon hours trolling through that book, looking at the synopsis of extremely rare TV shows, writing down the titles in the hope of one day being able to source them. Unfortunately we were never able to, thanks to the good old BBC wiping everything, but I think that time made us realise we had a lot in common.

Having this support meant everything to me. Suddenly I could make my own choices about what I did with my leisure time. For two hours, three times a week I knew I was free to do anything I wanted and I didn't have to wait for my Mum or Dad to be available. I used to long for these hours and like all great things, they would always go too fast once I'd showered, spent thirty minutes in my standing frame and did my homework. I wanted to get every last second out of my time with them. Forget PlayStation or Xbox, Steve and Calum were the best entertainment money could buy (well, for £3 per hour!)

My sometimes worrying fascination with Cilla Black would result in them doing things that were completely unimaginable. Designing television sets out of cardboard boxes I imagine wasn't what they had in mind when they agreed to help me out. However with Calum's warped imagination he always ensured that I could take a joke. For example when I created my first website on the history of British Comedy, Calum promptly transformed it into "Josh's page of dirty sluts" which consisted of lots of dubious images thrown together attempting to resemble my favourite comedians. Like brothers we were able to take the piss out of each other but I always knew that they had my back. Over the years Steve and Calum became friends and remained a loyal team for me throughout my teenage years.

You will be realising by now, that as a writer I am without real structure and it's actually unbelievable how this book has come together, because I am terrible at organising anything. Even my own birthday party, I was telling people the wrong time and restaurant to meet! But anyway, I digress… having this in mind it wouldn't surprise you that I have now decided to go back ten years to the start of school because Steve and Calum were not the first team that were able to shape my life.

When I was two and a half years old, during the microtechnology boom of the late 1980's (remember those massive mobile phones and computers that looked like something out of Star Trek? That was the epitome of Britain's IT back then), schools soon realised that they wanted in on the action and suddenly people were starting to think about how this new technology could benefit those with a severe disability. It was here that my whole family was introduced to another member of the JB Hall of Fame: Diane Godfree, a teacher who was working closely with Alice and Beryl to support disabled children with educational IT solutions. It was her mission to explore the possibilities of this new technology in relation to the capabilities of the many disabled children on the Isle of Wight. Diane (or Di) worked closely with my Mum, Alice and Beryl in order to drive the vision which would enable me to access a computer independently.

Di's determination even took the four of them on a trip to Oxford where they enrolled on a week-long course at the micro-technology centre. The centre was the first of its kind in the UK and supported children with disabilities who had problems accessing IT. (Think an old fashioned Apple Store for Crips!). Over five days they were able to witness success stories of those children who were a little like me and how they had overcome the obstacles of IT. Indeed, on their return it was agreed I should obtain a BBC computer with a very unique interface designed by Dr Carole Thornett of the micro-technology unit. Carole would prove to be a vital source to my computing requirements over the next fifteen years as she always remained at the forefront of technology and constantly created interfaces for disabled people. For her many advancements in technology, she was like Q from James Bond. Like any teenager it was my desire to own a Nintendo 64 in order to keep up with the activities of my friends. Carol was able to create a unique handset just for my sole purpose of using my N64. Despite my enthusiasm for the console, it was like asking a blind man for a game of snooker. (In the first draft I wrote "asking a bald man for a game of snooker" which gave the joke a much more sinister vibe than I had intended). I recall hours and hours spent attempting to complete the initial level of James Bond Goldeneye but Oddjob always shot me going through a corridor and I couldn't move my hand fast enough to escape. If only Nintendo made a game about Gladiators or Blind Date, I'd win every time!

Unfortunately, the funding for the IT scheme on the island came to an end and Di went on to use her experience as a teacher, and expertise in micro-technology, in other outlets. During this time, preparations were being made for my eventual primary education and it was agreed that Di would come on board as my individual support teacher. She would accompany my personal helper one morning a week to facilitate both my learning and the practicalities of me carrying out my school work. This proved to be a winning formula for my evolution as an academic and Di was able to remain as my individual support teacher for almost all of my school career. She helped shape both my personal and professional life into what it is today. Di wasn't just my teacher, at times she was my PA, my agent, my scribe, a trusted counsellor but above all one of my best friends. Over twenty-five years later, Di remains a vital part of my life and is always on hand to help me achieve and celebrate my many accomplishments. In short she has now become part of the family.

The other long-standing woman in my educational life came when we advertised in the local paper for a personal helper to assist me during my school day. Prior to this I had attended playschool which was located two minutes from where we lived. My parents thought it would be crucial for me not to be taken by my mum in order to offer some independence. For this, my mum employed a 19 year old college girl, Caroline Sheasby to take me. This gave me my first sense of freedom. For those hours I just felt like a normal 4 year old. It was here that I met one of my long-standing friends, Oliver Taylor. For the best part of a year myself and Oliver, it seemed, were inseparable and I often recall trying to roller skate down a footpath whilst he and my sister had gone on ahead and left me and Caroline behind. I couldn't even walk, let alone roller skate!

When it was time to go to school, Mum made the hard decision for Caroline not to continue working with me through fear that I would rely on her familiarity and not forge new relationships (I guess Mum didn't want me turning into my Dad, relying on one woman for everything!) It is only discussing this subject now with you, that I realise how much of a big call this was for my Mum to make. It would have been so easy for me and my whole family to become complacent with the fact that Caroline was always going to be there. Yet Mum has always been blessed with a wonderful sense of foresight and she knew that Caroline was already pregnant with her first son. Consequently she wasn't going to be in a physical condition that would allow her to continue to work with me (Mum didn't want her to be the subject of my feared, uncontrollable right hook from time to time). However, this did not stop Caroline's relationship with my family and again, more than twenty-five years on, we remain good friends.

So it was time to look for someone else… ah the unpredictable world of recruitment was something I was going to have to get used to. Who doesn't love a group of strangers going on about how they will change your life and the highlights of their sometimes relatively dull careers; it's great! Nowadays, if I wanted to put an advert out for a young women to fulfil all my physical needs it wouldn't be in the local paper. I'd either register for Tinder or graffiti it to cubicle number 4 of Cowes High Street toilets. I hear that's where the more desperate men pick up women. Looking back, the strange thing was all of the interviewees were women. But why women? This was the early 90's, not the 50's, but I think a lot of people still associated the field of care with women. This is ridiculous, what if I was a little prude? (Which I am definitely not!) I just can't believe no one even thought about it… I guess at the time no one figured it was important and why would they? But I still often wonder how different my experience would be if I had had a male helper just for the little things like being able to be together in swimming pool changing rooms or playing a sport.

However, when we did appoint a female candidate, it was my decision to select the very first one I met; a former playgroup leader called Penny Waters. Unbeknown to all, Penny would also become part of the family and for over fourteen years she helped to shape my life. Penny never asked for praise or stole the limelight, instead she attempted to be totally invisible and created an environment where it became possible for both staff and students to interact with me. Whatever I did, wherever I went, Penny was quick to follow.

Naturally sporty and competitive, she was great at involving me in a whole range of different activities from football to rounders. Although being of a similar generation to Mum and Dad, Penny was able to get the perfect balance between being an advocate for my independence while still maintaining a united front with my parents. She understood that I wanted to be just one of the crowd and never "snitched" on me or my peers. To her, she was just my enabler and in order to do this she also needed my friends to trust her in the same way as they trusted me… And for fourteen years they did! Never calling her Miss or Mrs Murton, it was just Penny and that's definitely how I liked it.

As I got older and my sense of humour became ever more dark and twisted, Penny was the perfect foil to my outlandish behaviour. I recall one day on a visit to the hydrotherapy pool, Penny was struck with a bad case of stomach ache and in the changing room she let out what could only be described as an atomic bomb! As someone who always presented herself suitably for any occasion, bloody hell she had some guts on her. Trust me it was the worst fart I have ever smelt! Sorry Penny, but had to tell it. I hope you've recovered now.

Di and Penny made the perfect team in supporting both my educational and physical needs. As I began to cultivate my interest in the art of writing, they were both able to find techniques and situations in order to bring my creative talents to the fore. Crucially, instead of playing on the activities and lessons which I couldn't do, they concentrated on the things I could.

They not only became experts in my own style of learning but were able to have a dominant influence on my life. Both of them understood that in order to achieve my potential as a student they needed to support me with every aspect of my life, irrespective of whether it came into their job specification or not. It was 360° support and this custom style of learning had a very positive effect on me. I always knew that whatever was going on and however I felt, I would always be accounted for by these two special women. So, when they found hard-core porno magazines at the top of my bag which my mates had deliberately put there, instead of questioning me about them they just carefully folded them up and stuck them back in my bag and waited for the appropriate moment for me to look through them... you could never say they didn't promote equal opportunities! Indeed, I would like to think it was not just a job to them, more a way of life. In short, they both went a long way to making me the man I am and over fifteen years later they remain vital players within my life.

There's a lot more to come about my education but as I'm prone to skip about I'm going to jump ahead a fair while.

Just like Man United discovered when Alex Ferguson retired, replicating a long-standing partnership is very hard to do. I was unlikely to find this devotion ever again and I'm not sure how that made me feel. I'd had carers come and go but Di and Penny had been constants in my life for well over a decade. They created a safe little nest where I could flourish and suddenly it was taken away.

Yet I had a vision (not a dream, for all you Luther King fans!). I was determined to get through university just like all my mates. I was bright enough, I was strong enough and this was a part of my life which I was adamant my disability would not dictate. If it meant being patient while the university got to grips with my educational requirements then that's what I would do. All I knew was, I was going to Bournemouth University and would have gone to the ends of the earth to get there!

It took a long time to recreate this feeling of Di and Penny's utter devotion, but two new people were about to show up. On first arriving at Uni I was living in disabled accommodation, I felt like a bit of a spare part to be honest. I wasn't used to being the outsider looking at everyone else having fun. Yet for the first year I could not find a way of integrating myself into any group. By welcoming me into their lives, Steve and Gray gave me a new facet to my University experience and offered me a reason to call Bournemouth my home. Suddenly I could go and tell my school friends about funny antics I got up to with Steve and Gray. I was no longer subject to seven nights of television per week. I could go to the pub with a crowd of like-minded people and have a laugh. I'd finally found a life for myself in Bournemouth and it felt great.

It didn't take long for me to realise that the three of us were extremely similar in our lifestyle choices: we all liked to stay up late sampling rum and vodka (I use the term "sampling" in the very loosest sense!). To top it off it was discovered very quickly that we all shared the same twisted sense of humour, which was a great thing for us but bad for everyone who stepped foot in our flat and became absolutely bewildered as to the bizarre conversations which took place. I particularly recall one occasion on returning from the Christmas holidays; I'd been bought a head massager and Gray promptly saw this as the perfect opportunity to freak out my support worker John, by placing the head massager on his head for an uncomfortable amount of time... extremely childish but very funny!

When the madness, drinking and hard work of university was over, I was faced with a life back on the Isle of Wight. But before I could make my Dirty Den styled return, I needed a new team of poor, unfortunate helpers who didn't know what they had let themselves in for. When we recruited James Hudson, a nineteen year old college graduate he agreed to come to Bournemouth and see how it was done by Gray. James was more than capable of continuing this bizarre nature in which I like to live. Over the years he has been forced to increasingly cope with my frequent surreal behaviour like when I chose to perform a routine about midgets at a Stand-Up Comedy class and he had to translate in his own unique style. Whatever I've done, James has been the perfect companion.

Being my helper at such a pivotal stage of my life wasn't easy. Managing my professional aspirations alongside providing me with wrap around personal care is no easy task. Fresh from university, I lacked direction but was conscious that I needed to be productive. I somehow thought that graduating with a Masters I would automatically be inundated with project requests and opportunities. Yet it's a bitter pill to swallow when you wake up to an empty email inbox and nobody replies to your letters. James has assisted me in adapting the work I do so that I can achieve a sense of fulfilment whilst being realistic about my career opportunities. I would really love to take a junior researcher's position at the BBC but the logistics would be too impractical. James is only too aware of this constant struggle between the life that I want and the life that I've got and is one of the few people who can truly help me overcome this hurdle.

This is not to say that James is the perfect carer, as it has been known for onlookers to compare our relationship to that of an old married couple where we spend fifty percent of everyday bickering and we both know exactly how to irritate one another within a second. Affectionately known as 'Big Guns' to my whole family, James is the perfect complement to my frequent outlandish behaviour and I love exploring new ways to terrorise him and make him feel very uncomfortable. Someone once described James as like a puppy, you need to gain his trust but once provoked, he barks.

It was a strange feeling being back at home. When I was at Uni, I used to look forward to weekends and holidays back on the Island but now the novelty had worn off. I began to long for that independence that I had at Bornemouth and found it very hard to adjust to Mum and Dad's evening routine. Obviously with both of them having full time jobs, their evenings were spent watching television or getting an early night. As a night owl, this would frustrate me but I knew if I was under their roof I would have to play by their rules. If only there was a way of playing by my own rules again. This feeling culminated in the selection of a new carer, 18-year old George Gard, a former Ice Hockey player who could fill any doorway. The size of a giant but with the spirit of a Dalmatian, George perfectly complemented my care team and made me realise that moving out wasn't a pipe dream, it could actually be a reality. I'm saying this like George was some sort of philosopher, he wasn't. Anyone who comes out with the line 'Could you walk when you were born?' Or 'Jimmy Tarbuck? Was he in the Two Ronnies?' has to be someone very, very special indeed.

Together with James and 'The Giant' (It sounds like a title of a Roald Dahl book!) I was able to think more creatively about what I wanted to get out of life. This involved moving into my own bungalow. For some reason I always assumed this would be impossible and even though I had lived away from home for four years, I always thought that Mum, Dad and I would roll around in our big family house forever. I suppose it would have been interesting if I had actually managed to defy the odds and met a woman who had been "up for it". It would have been highly embarrassing if I had to speak through the intercom and ask my dad to put me on and take me off… Just think about that for a moment… it's not exactly ideal is it?!

On a serious note, realising my limitations and differences has definitely been the hardest thing in my life. When you're a twin of an able-bodied sibling it is easy to measure the differences between the two of you. As babies, everyone always tells us that me and Soph were inseparable and became really protective of one another. My mum regularly recalls taking me for a check-up at the hospital when I started screaming and became agitated. All of a sudden my mum looked round to see Soph hitting the doctor with her child's rucksack, making the doctor protect himself. It was clear that even as a little child Soph was very protective of me. She still is.

With this being said the mere fact that she was able-bodied intrinsically meant that she was able to thrive on the freedom of growing up. Something that I could never do. To me, this didn't add up. It was like having a window on the world; I knew I couldn't be a part of it but I could see the carrot of independence dangling in front of my face. Sometimes life isn't fair and occasionally I felt I had a rough deal.

As I said before, I wrote this book to show the positive sides of disability of which there are many (such as clipboard warriors in the high street, never wanting to ask me for a donation or 'moment of my time'). However, in order to convey a three dimensional image of what it's like having such a disability, I hope you can appreciate me having to discuss a few of the negative points. In this situation, I often wonder if my beliefs about disability are justified. Integrating with able-bodied people is great but coming to terms with your limitations is difficult when all the people around you have no idea what you're going through. If you're reading this feeling in a similar situation; I'd love to say it gets easier over time and it does. Yet, occasionally, you still get periods where it's all you think about. I find that if I surround myself with upbeat people who make me feel like I can do anything, this feeling doesn't last as long as it once did.

As I've grown up I've learnt to regard these feelings not as limitations, more just something I have to get through in order to make the most of the good times. This is where my twin, Soph and older sister, Lauren come into their own in helping me engage with people who may otherwise be uncomfortable being in my presence. Once strangers realise that I am able to contribute to any social situation, most of them become comfortable with interacting with me in their own right.

You may be thinking this was a great thing for Lauren and Soph to do. After all, they were only kids themselves and to be mindful of my requirements at such a young age, I guess shows an enormous generosity of spirit on their part. But for me at the time, I wanted to prove to myself that I could make friends without intervention from Lauren and Soph, without someone else talking people round and telling them "Josh is just a normal guy". To me, friends should not be coerced into liking you, it should naturally evolve over time and that's what I wanted to do.

Growing up with two sisters I've realised that most women need to have constant dialogue with others in order to feel part of a gang. I don't think it's like that with men. I feel for men it's about quality over quantity. We can have a good night out that will satisfy that social urge for at least a couple of months. Women are just more sociable and Lauren and Soph have always had a thriving social life. When we were younger I used to worry about not seeing my friends as regularly as they did, but now I realise that is down to this 'social need' divide between men and women. So roll on the FA Cup Final!

Turning thirty made me realise that as you get older people don't crave the thrill of being all together all the time. Instead you enjoy other pleasures; nice food, a good film, playing board games with the family (Christ, now I sound old!). This is perhaps the only area in which I feel on par with the average Joe. Everyone gets their own responsibilities and other priorities have to take precedence. As someone who loves a good night out and feels just as 'at home' in the pub, I have been forced to find other people to have that all important pint with. However, I believe that friendship is like a beautiful piece of art. Sometimes less is more.

In a funny sort of way, I sometimes believe that I have always been and always will be a very sociable person. I thrive on the ecstasy of interacting with a whole host of different people, whether it's a large group down the pub or a room full of spectators witnessing one of my new projects, I love being with people. It's what gets me through the dark times and makes me look forward to the good times.

So how do I sum up this chapter? I've talked about everything from spastics on roller-skates to hard-core pornography! But I haven't done it alone. I need people around me to do just about everything and this isn't always easy to perfect but when it is, I'm sure you can imagine it is the best thing on this earth! Maybe I can't unscrew the lid off a bottle of Heinz Ketchup or put a photo on the wall but does that matter? …not really.

III

The Sun Always Shines on TV

If you're a fan of A-ha! Then I'm afraid you might be a bit disappointed by this chapter as it has absolutely nothing to do with the band or the song. In fact it's just a nice segue to talk about my love for TV, so if you're waiting for a chapter called "Take on me", I'm afraid you have the wrong book and even if I did decide to write that chapter, I don't think you'd want to read it!

Now then, this chapter is going to be a little different from the last, in fact this and the following chapter could make up their own separate book. Most of this book is about me getting on with life irrespective of my challenges. However, if you don't know a bit about what I do with my life, you won't fully understand the emotional journey that I've been on in order to achieve my career aspirations.

Having Cerebral Palsy, people have always been mindful of the activities I could get involved with and whilst I was a gutsy child who wanted to give everything a go, I was still very aware of my limitations. So, whenever I had a passion for something, it was always extremely encouraged in order to give me a sense of fulfilment, which others could get from a football or a tennis racket. For some reason every time I saw a television, I was instantly hooked. Not because I had what is today diagnosed as "Screen Addiction" by right wing educational campaigners, it was more that I was struck by this small box in the corner of the sitting room that had the power to entertain and, more importantly, inspire. I might not have been able to kick a football or ride a bike but watching television was one of the only activities I could fully enjoy. It didn't need me to be able to stay on my feet for hours and hours nor did I need any special equipment in order to do it. This was the only section of my life that didn't need adapting in order for me to take part. I could do it just like any Tom, Dick or Harry!

Thus began a passion for the history of Light Entertainment, which has influenced the whole body of my work. I sometimes feel that in a funny sort of way this has defined me more than my Cerebral Palsy. I wasn't only fascinated by the aesthetics of television but was desperate to find out how it was made. Suddenly I had found my own version of a bat and ball and it felt great! Light Entertainment became my ecstasy and from then on it was my aim to enter this wonderful and magical world.

How was I going to do this? I couldn't even make myself understood to a room full of friends, let alone the public. I could simply have forgotten about the idea forever, but that's not me, I can never give up and let my CP get the better of me... that's definitely not who I am! Granted I was never going to be the next Bruce Forsyth but I could still research and write about the art of performing, which went some way to satisfying the hidden entertainer in me (ooh, darling!).

This fascination began at the tender age of five, when I sat down with my family to watch the 1993 Royal Variety Performance. Now I know what you're thinking, "Bloody hell, he's some sort of theatrical diva, like a flamboyant Stephen Hawking…" well I sort of am! If only Louie Spence did the voice for speech aids! Anyway, 1993 was the year that Blind Date was riding high in the television schedule and a certain Cilla Black was celebrating her 30th anniversary in show business. To mark such an occasion she was put forward as the host of the annual Royal Variety at the Dominion Theatre, London. I can remember it like it was yesterday. It was like something out of my dreams! So many performers in one place and for the very first time I realised that Cilla Black was not just the presenter of Blind Date, she was a very accomplished and indeed prestigious performer and entertainer. This encouraged me to follow her career to areas which I had never been before.

During my first year at school, the parents were warned of an upcoming book day when all children would have the opportunity to dress up as their favourite character from a book. My sister, Soph had already decided that she was going to dress up as her namesake from a series of horse riding books, which she read avidly in the months leading up to the event. However, when Mum asked me what character I would like to dress up as, before she had a chance to open her dressing up box for the second time, I replied, 'Cilla Black'. She promptly had a terrible moment where she thought, 'Not only is my son heavily disabled but he also has a fascination with middle-aged northern women.' At least that would have claimed victory when playing Dysfunctional Top Trumps. But this was no laughing matter, how was she going to make me a Cilla Black costume in one night? I eventually turned up at school the next day in a ginger wig, wearing an old pair of floral curtains which Mum had made into a dress and a pair of my Mum's high heels which kept falling off my wheelchair step, much to Penny's annoyance. I can't remember much about that day, though I suppose I must have got worrying looks from parents and children alike.

At this stage I would really like to suggest that this was a once in a lifetime occurrence, however after my Mum had made that costume I would dress up in the evening, walk in to the garden and insist on re-enacting an episode of Blind

Date with myself playing the part of Cilla of course. I guess this was my first taste of creating my own media, something which I would improve on in later years and despite no longer dressing up as Cilla Black (thankfully) I still have the drive and ambition to become a media auteur. This has not stopped my Mum from elaborating on the story. Every time she is asked to tell it, she adds a final element of embarrassment, surrounding her placing a pair of footballs up my top so I could become Dawn French, but that is definitely a big fat lie!

My interest in such a figure as Cilla would subsequently introduce me to the unique and enigmatic world of show business and although Ms Black may have quite a specific audience, my interest opened me up to a whole environment of endless opportunities. Whilst following Cilla's work I was able to become familiar with the many stars she had become associated with during her long and distinguished career, including a handful of legendary comedians such as Jimmy Tarbuck, Bruce Forsyth and Frankie Howerd. This gave me a grounding from which to appreciate other performers of this era. Even at that young age I recognised that the older generation of performers seemed to have a more intimate relationship with the British public (some got more intimate than others!) and treated them as old friends rather than a training ground for new material. In short, you always knew what you were getting. Thus began my passion for the golden era of British entertainment which in my opinion ran from 1951-1975.

This opened up a whole new world for me as there seemed to be an endless amount of stars and television shows for me to discover in my quest to find all the pieces of the British entertainment jigsaw. So rich and diverse, the entertainment industry is packed with fascinating stories about how the medium evolved. I still find it fascinating when I discover a new gem of information that I didn't know. You could say I am a British Entertainment geek but I love it!

As great as it was researching the diverse world of Light Entertainment, I still had a real hankering to be part of it myself. I needed something that would elevate me into the performance arena, where I so wanted to be. However, directing and producing seemed to lack the glitz and glamour of the entertainers who had drawn me into this world of show business originally.

An ironic thing is, I constantly get told that I am extremely gobby for someone who can't speak very well, so I figured if I couldn't say it, then I could surely write it down for someone else to say. That is essentially what scriptwriting is! I've always loved sitcoms and the art of dialogue, so it didn't take me long to realise that scriptwriting could be an area which I could have a go at! Then I discovered a script writer was living in the local area and taught classes on the art of screen writing. Although I was far too young to be considered eligible for such classes, it gave me something to channel my aspirations towards and made me reflect on whether this indeed was the art for me.

At the age of thirteen my Mum approached this local screen writer, Jeremy Davis, regarding the possibility of tutoring me for a ten-week course in preparation of me writing my first twenty-four minute situation comedy. To my delight he accepted my Mum's offer and thus commenced a flourishing working relationship with myself, Steve and Di, who would all be present for one hour a week. Although very basic in its approach, Jeremy's script writing lessons would prove to be vital to my evolution as a screen writer and equipped me with an understanding of the art which I would nurture in years to come.

My association with Jeremy would last until my inevitable path to university. Under his instruction and influence I was able to write a further thirty minute drama which I would later refine and elongate as the major project for my under graduate course. Jeremy also volunteered his services to help me in school as a relief teacher, in the event that Penny or Di were unavailable. However, only a couple of weeks into this new agreement, tragedy struck as Jeremy was diagnosed with a fast and aggressive form of cancer. Sadly, this was a battle that even the most intelligent among us could not win and not long after his last session with me, he passed away, leaving a whole gallery of accreditations and creative masterpieces in his legacy.

I often stop and think about Jeremy and the positive effect he had on my early progress as a writer. I only wish he had survived long enough to help me celebrate my many successes and often wonder as to the advice he would be able to give me now. The work I did with him bore no connection with my disability, it was just my imagination and that's what I loved about it. The feeling that I could take my work in any direction I chose was so rewarding and Jeremy always took me for what I was and not the sweet boy in the wheelchair. He identified with my dreams and aspirations and just wanted to help me achieve them. Irrespective of how successful I may become as a writer, or which area of creative writing I may find myself within during the years to come, Jeremy Davies will always play a very significant role in my evolution as a writer. May he rest in peace.

I remember calling myself a writer when I hadn't actually written many scripts. I thought it made me sound interesting and when people asked me what I was working on, I would come out with these awful ideas about people in hotels or a northern family watching TV… You can see I wasn't very original! The funny thing was that after the first term of my Masters, I came home with a comedy script and gave it to my Dad to read, to which he replied, "It's good, but it's not as good as that Royle Family one you wrote when you were at school." I'm still debating if this was the biggest insult I've ever had! Looking back over the scripts I wrote in my teens, I sometimes wince at the infantile and innocent nature of the pieces and indeed the development of my individual voice. I was definitely not an Alan Bennett yet!

I think you'll agree that going from Cilla Black to Alan Bennett is a massive jump… even for this book which you probably have gathered by now is a little bit random! I always thought that scriptwriting was at the heart of showbiz, where it all happened, but it's not. Scriptwriters are mostly lonely men and women sat in front of a blank screen, drinking coffee and getting frustrated as to why there are so few pages in their Word document. The scriptwriter is a word minimiser but a page maximiser. Each character has to have their own voice which is unique to only them and has to contribute something to moving the story on. Being in a room with a scriptwriter in full flow would be a psychiatrist's dream.

Writers usually tend to be totally isolated from the enigmatic world of the studio and only takes ownership over their work during the time it takes to create it. If I had known this fact when I was in the initial stages of my development I would have given up on day one. Nevertheless, once I had got to grips with the techniques of the art, I knew there was no going back. I had the scriptwriting bug.

My ambitions in scriptwriting have always lain within the intimate nature of the small screen. I get bored watching a film and normally fall asleep in the cinema. To me, Rocky is a chocolate biscuit! I actually hate those people at parties who go around saying "Have you seen the latest 'Fast and Furious' film? It's so much better than the previous one…" The only thing 'Fast and Furious' they need to worry about is my middle finger! So you can imagine my delight when I enrolled on my scriptwriting degree and discovered that everyone loved film. I quickly realised that in terms of film, I was out of my depth. I remember thinking, "I'm sure David Lean is a really lovely guy but who is he?" It seemed worlds apart from the work I did with Jeremy and I wasn't sure if I was going to like the constant dominance of film. I also realised that I was the youngest student on the course in a lecture theatre full of students who differed vastly in age and experience.

You may be thinking how do you do a three year undergraduate course just on the art of scriptwriting? To be honest, I had the same thoughts when I enrolled. It's not like studying a Science Degree where there is always a categorical right or wrong answer, this was a lot more subjective and a lot of the content was heavily influenced by the passions of the teaching staff. Therefore, instead of learning about a broad range of media themes, we were rather the victims of theoretical elitism (or Film Nazi's, as I called them)! I got on well with most of the staff and they soon realised my bizarre interest in sixties and seventies television, which was mocked on a regular basis. But I knew that as the majority of the others in the group were all film buffs, there was very little I could do about it. It felt like a different world. I remember thinking Britain has such a rich cultural history and all you want to do is talk about experimental American tat. It was just a shame!

This was the predicament I found myself in throughout my four years at Bournemouth University. Yet what did I do? If everyone else was absolutely loving the content, I didn't really have a leg to stand on (not even a wheel to sit on). I didn't want to make myself look as pretentious as some of the others in the group, who wore long black overcoats and had strangely bizarre opinions about the state of Pixar (I thought Pixar was something Dizzee Rascal said!). But none of it seemed to get my juices flowing. I was waiting for that something that I could really get passionate about, that thing that really appealed to my creativity and love for the art (now I sound pretentious!). But it never really came, unless it was in a one-on-one tutorial where I could really tell the staff what it was that made me want to be a writer.

For this reason, I never actually found a middle ground with most of my peers. You would think on a degree as specific as scriptwriting, everyone would have the same agenda so it would be easy to get along with people. But I clearly did not understand where they were coming from and I imagine they felt the same about me. A dribbling spastic with a weird fascination for old British television wouldn't exactly make you want to start a conversation would it?

Yet it was definitely not all bad. I may not have liked the theoretical component but the practical aspect was right up my alley. Throughout my first year I was lucky enough to have a tutor who very much reflected my aspirations in script writing. Comedy writer and "wide boy" Jan Weddup, realised my love for the bizarre and was determined to help me refine my flair for comedy. Weddup was a unique individual, somewhere between Shakespeare and Frank Butcher (is that libellous?).

Over the first year of university my relationship with Jan Weddup blossomed. He was quick to recognise my extensive knowledge of British comedy when I regularly found it necessary to correct him on a few vital statistics. On one occasion he was holding a seminar on situation comedy and was giving examples of the BBC's dominance within this genre and used Only Fools and Horses, Dad's Army and Till Death Us Do Part as examples. In an instant I raised my hand and gave him a sarcastic look, he replied with the one word, "Barry?" to which I replied, "I think you're wrong there." Putting the white board marker down on the table he looked intently at me and so did the rest of the group. I said, "Till Death Us Do Part was an ITV production." He looked at me, placed his glasses on the edge of his nose and said, "Pardon?" My educational access assistant felt the need to repeat my utterance for both clarifications and dramatic effect. Weddup went over to his notes and wrote something down. "I'll make a note of that," he said. On returning to my flat I checked my inbox and discovered an email from Weddup which read, "I have just checked on the international movie and television database, and Till Death Us Do Part began on the BBC in 1965 and switched to ITV in the 70's, so we are both right…" That was the pinnacle of my relationship with such a wonderful and unique man. It would be safe to say that he never argued with me again, or me with him!

If my university experience was a re-enactment of Star Wars, then Jan Weddup was definitely Obi-Wan Kenobi to my Luke Skywalker. He was able to teach me the integral balance between work and play. I recall one day he knocked on my front door and said, "I need a word." A lot of things were going through my mind, had I failed my first year? Was there something wrong with my assignment? Was he kicking me off the course? He came in, sat down and said, "I'm worried you're not having that much fun." He then told me the importance of alcohol to your work and said that I needed to start enjoying myself a bit more. This was a lecturer telling me to have a jolly, I couldn't believe what I was hearing! Throughout the succeeding years whenever I had a cause for complaint, Weddup was always in residence ready to fight my corner. On one particular occasion I found myself having issues with an educational assistant. When Jan discovered this, he found it necessary to take a stand. Even though he was no longer my personal tutor, he thought this was cause for concern and stepped in to support me. If his involvement had not been so dominant I may never have gotten through Uni.

The other major influence on both my writing and creative style came in my second year, when I attended a free writing seminar led by John Foster. Foster is a creative type who believes in the improvisation side of learning. There is never a right or wrong answer and if a writer can access their subconscious with the work they create, he believes it will make them a better writer. The key to this is free-writing; the technique of writing for ten minutes non-stop devoid of any structure or meaning, in short it's like written down verbal diarrhoea! Not having discovered how to write with my nose on an iPad yet, I relied on scribing for my whole Uni work. SO, how the hell was I meant to do this? I must say that I'm not one of those disabled people who thinks everyone should know about my needs as if by magic, and I don't feel the need to write it on my t-shirt, but if I have an opportunity I want to make the most of it, I'm not there just to sit and watch.

In the following days the additional learning support department issued a complaint to Foster on the grounds that his seminar was not inclusive. Admittedly I did feel slightly sorry for John as if he hadn't been warned about me and my situation then how was he expected to tailor the session accordingly? My initial reaction was to forget about it, and carry out the task in my own time. I then received an email from Foster inviting me to an hour and a half one-on-one tutorial whereupon he offered me the same experience as my peers. In addition to this, he offered me extra exercises to enhance and influence my technique in character development and then organised a follow up tutorial where I would have the opportunity to exhibit my work. Suddenly this seemed a better experience than what had taken place during the seminar.

From this point on, John realised that he had to be mindful of my ability to participate in activities and became one of the most inclusive tutors in my whole time at university. He knew that these writing exercises were one of my favourite aspects of the course and always ensured that I had the same experiences as everyone else. If this meant booking two seminar rooms so I had adequate space to complete the activities without distraction, then that's what needed to happen. It was still exactly the same seminar, just adapted so everyone could join in. In these circumstances I didn't feel any different from anyone else. To me, this was exactly what university was about!

One could only imagine my delight when I returned to university for my third year and discovered that my tutor was indeed John Foster. However, this was tinged with the sad news that Jan Weddup had retired. He wouldn't be giving potential creative types the benefit of his wealth of experience or the encouragement that I had been lucky enough to obtain. His support and supervision had been the perfect introduction to university life and bridged the gap between my school and university education, I couldn't believe that I wouldn't be able to have regular banter with him anymore… it somehow felt strange.

Despite Weddup's departure, my relationship with John Foster continued to flourish and my third year at university was deemed a success by my first attempt at writing a feature film. For this I returned to a story idea which had been conceived during my time with Jeremy Davies. It centred on a man in his twilight years reigniting his feelings for his former wife whom he had not seen for over two decades. I know what you're thinking, how the hell did I know anything about a man in his twilight years? Well, all my friends say that I am like an old man so I had a bit of empathy there. The development of the piece was the most fascinating research I have ever conducted as it concerned what kept people together and the feelings that they still had for their first love. In order to get a rounded image of the story, I needed to find out what it was like to have a long relationship so I began to interview those who I knew well. This was the first time I had interviewed people and was surprised at their reaction to my questions. Some became really emotional when they started to recount tales of their past. This is where I realised the power of the interview and it was something that I was interested to follow up. This was the major factor in me obtaining a 2-2 for my degree.

Like almost everything in my life, I took my degree day by day and didn't stop and think about my achievement. I always find I work better when I don't think about the bigger picture or the purpose of what I'm doing. Without even realising, I'd finished my degree and although at the time I just felt relieved, it's only when I look back that I realise the massive achievement it was. For a child who had to fight so hard to get into mainstream school, this was the ultimate two fingers up to everyone who said I couldn't do it. But beyond that, I'd done myself so proud!

It was in the middle of the third term that John Foster revealed he was thinking of creating a Master's degree centred on different forms of writing. I had never considered undertaking a Masters as I felt that it was more important to create a portfolio of work which would have more weight when tackling potential employers. In fact the BBC sometimes are reluctant to take on media graduates as a result of the theoretical nature in which they are taught. However, after discussing this new course with John, I realised that it might cover some of the content which I thought my BA lacked and decided to enrol.

I couldn't wait! The feeling that I could finally get my teeth stuck into something worthwhile again got me really excited. On my arrival I discovered that a lot of the content was similar to my BA yet I was older and wiser. I knew that I would just have to do my own thing and make the most of having resources at my fingertips. As a Master's student I was far more aware of what you needed to survive the course and was no longer a bystander but a veteran of university life.

When the major project was announced it was stated that we could either write a portfolio of different writing styles with a very definite common theme or we could write a feature length screen play. Originally I was going to opt for the portfolio as I surmised that I had already created a feature length screenplay for my BA. However, only a few days into the project, I had a great epiphany to write a biographical drama based on the life and work of Bill Cotton. Now here is where I get a bit of an anorak… are you ready? Here goes… Sir William Frederick "Bill" Cotton CBE, was the Head of Light Entertainment at the BBC between 1969 and 1977. He nurtured the TV careers of many of our best loved performers such as Morecambe and Wise, The Two Ronnies and Michael Parkinson. Some say he created the 'golden era' in British Entertainment. Phew! You can breathe now.

Part of my research for the film was to obtain witness accounts from the many celebrities of that era. As a fan of vintage television I was in my element as I had the opportunity to speak with and sometimes meet my heroes of this genre. These included; Barry Cryer, Ray Galton and Alan Simpson, Angela Rippon and Nicholas Parsons. For somebody like myself who is so interested in this era of British television it was unbelievable and made me realise even more that this was the world I wanted to be in. This is where I used my disability to its full advantage and played on it to open a lot of doors which normally would have remained shut. A Cerebral Palsy sufferer undertaking a Masters somehow seemed more admirable than just a normal spotty twenty-two year old!

Get ready… a bit more anorak shit coming up! Bill Cotton's tenure at the BBC coincided with the corporation slowly realising the power of television and the impact it had on the nation. Arguably he created the first crop of nationwide television stars and "Must-see TV". For me this was fascinating, as I was essentially researching a story that I thought I knew well but in a completely different way. It just felt like everything I was passionate about had all come together. It was like one big celebration and it seemed unbelievable that this would be what would eventually gain me a Master's Degree.

When I returned home, an attempt was made to get the script read by a number of different companies who may have been interested in taking it further. However, as a result of the subject matter it became a little more complicated to offer the finished piece around than I had anticipated, due to loyalties, both to the Cotton family and the BBC. At present, there does not seem to be a way of making it look appealing to a reliable broadcaster. Yet I remain hopeful that in the years to come, the television climate may change and there will be a place for it on the small screen. For now, the script makes a tidy ornament on my book case.

So I think you'll agree that I have come a long way from those early days and my fascination with Cilla Black! I am just very thankful that I have been blessed with the drive and ambition to do anything I put my mind to. Yes I have Cerebral Palsy, but I'll never let that get in the way of achieving my hopes and aspirations.

As most people do in their lives, I've had many ups and downs in mine, but one thing has remained and that is my love for British entertainment. Hopefully it will continue to flourish into whatever guise I choose. So don't turn off your television set.

IV

The Trials of TV

Congratulations for getting to the fourth chapter. I suppose this part of the story is about my ambitions to enter into the world of showbiz. The last chapter was essentially about my hopes and dreams in entertainment, this is about how I made those dreams a reality. People are always criticising me for devaluing my projects and not being proud of where I am, but for me, I believe I have a lot left to achieve before I feel that magical sense of success. However, the following tale is about me trying to do just that.

I'm often told that I should be about 75 years old to have the sort of taste in entertainment that I do. Even to this day I'm not really sure where it comes from. Alice always referred to it as an "indescribable interest" and one she was never able to get to the bottom of. Yet irrespective of the reasons behind it, I have always set my sights on a life within the Arts. It's the only thing I've ever wanted to do (well, except being Jo Whiley's personal masseuse but you can't have everything can you?!).

Action figures are a common staple of nearly all boys' childhoods. Whether it's Action Man, Stretch Armstrong or some other would-be Disney hero. But there's one other range of figures, those bizarre large headed footballers which they seem to make every time England qualify for a major tournament. You know, the ones that find themselves at the bottom of the bargain bin at the precise moment when we are knocked out! Like the crap toys you used to get inside cereal packets, these figures are possibly a nice momentum for the tournament but when it's over they are thrown away or put out for the jumble sale. However, for me, all these types of figures, even the rubbish ones, were more than this; as a child they were the perfect way for me to start creating my own brand of entertainment.

Each figure was attributed to a famous face on British television as I went about developing and creating my take on the programmes that I watched. Terry Wogan aptly fitted the features of Wolf from Gladiators, Cilla Black became April O'Neil of The Teenage Mutant Ninja Turtles and Michael Parkinson doubled up as Rick Flair from WWF. If any of these high-profile stars ever discovered who I had chosen as their plastic doppelgänger, I expect I would have found myself with a lawsuit on my hands! But for the next fifteen years this pastime would continue to occupy me for hours and hours on end.

This has long been the source of hilarity for my family, whenever I meet a famous person they always insist on reminding me which figure that celebrity represented. In 1996 when we went to Radio 1 to meet Chris Evans, my Mum thought it would be funny to bring the figure I had labelled as his alter-ego, which was Egon Spengler from Ghostbusters. Even though I was a mere nine-years old, I was able to stun the ever-vocal Evans into complete silence. Luckily for me he didn't sue!

Irrespective of the uncomplimentary nature in which I attributed celebrities to the action figures, it still provided me with enjoyment and as I grew older, my ideas for shows that I created inside my cardboard box became ever more complex. While Soph and my mates were out skateboarding, playing pogs or kicking a football around, I was in my bedroom acting out television shows with my plastic figures. This was the only activity where I didn't care about being different because I could create whatever I wanted. For my tenth birthday, my Gran commissioned a dolls house creator to make me my very own toy theatre together with a Royal Box and two sets of curtains. Without a doubt, this was the best present that I have ever been given and I got an enormous amount of enjoyment out of it, until it eventually disintegrated leaving me with no option but to return to the reliable cardboard box.

As the new millennium dawned, the content which I created with these plastic figures grew ever more elaborate and complex. I devised television schedules which I played out inside the parameters of the cardboard box. Such schedules bore a similarity to Comic Relief and Children in Need which spanned four or five days of air time (I expect this would be enough to bankrupt the BBC!). They were mostly hosted by Michael Parkinson or Terry Wogan and would involve these "mature" stars being on air for several hours at a time. Luckily for them I never made it to Director of Programmes during their televisual supremacy.

By the time I reached university, my days of "playing" with cardboard boxes were numbered, so I directed my passion and enthusiasm to writing about the world of Light Entertainment. I realised that I could not only research the history of the business but I could even meet and interview some of my heroes. It wasn't until I reached university that I discovered that it would indeed be possible to create a dialogue between me and the people who I always thought were so unreachable. I always felt that these stars lived in a totally different world from me and there was no way that I could even dream to meet some of my heroes. However, if university taught me anything it was that no one is ever untouchable and outside of contact.

My third year of university meant only one thing: a dissertation. At the end of the second year, the whole media framework fraternity sat in the main lecture theatre to decide upon our thesis. By this time, I had already been resigned to the fact that my dissertation would be extremely different from the consensus of my year group as a result of my love for television. I didn't much care about the dynamics of Pixar or the history of the Cohen Brothers franchise. Then it came to me like a bolt of lightning: I had made a decision! The title of my dissertation was: "A Freudian View of Women in 1970's Sitcom". I know what you're thinking, "a little bizarre" but I'm sure you have realised by now that left field is in my nature!

For the research of such a mammoth project I realised that I was going to need to read a great deal of literature to form the backbone of my work. I started by reading Missing Believed Wiped by television consultant, Dick Fiddy who works closely with the British Film Institute (BFI), because I remembered I'd watched the BBC Four series which he'd spearheaded. The programme fascinated me with the way that Dick and the team tracked down lost archive footage from the BBC. As a fan of vintage British television, I could see the importance of this initiative and maybe if this concept had been created years previously, I could have enjoyed more of the programmes from yesteryear.

On opening the book, I noticed that Mr Fiddy's email address appeared alongside the publisher's details. Not being one to miss an opportunity, I quickly asked my assistant to make a note of the email address and then I sent him a polite message telling him all about me and my dissertation. To my amazement he swiftly replied with a detailed account of his view on the role of women in British sitcoms, which was at least three of four pages long. I couldn't believe it! I'd been watching him on television for years and now Dick Fiddy himself was emailing me! This was the first time that anyone famous had had a direct involvement in my work and I was just glowing with pride.

My dissertation made me realise that I am at my most productive when I have projects which I feel passionate about. Like any writer, I know what makes me tick and what makes me have that urge to get out of bed in the morning. I loved 1970's sitcom and had studied the work of Sigmund Freud for A level, so I already knew a little about the basis of his theories. All that was needed was a link between the two.

For some reason, whenever I'm in need of assistance, people are always very obliging and bend over backwards to help me. I just feel so lucky to have this reassuring assistance and without it, it would be impossible to know where I would be. In this instance, it was my former Philosophy and Ethics teacher John Featherstone. I clearly remember Mr Featherstone spending hours and hours explaining the theory behind Freud's Oedipus Complex and his belief that religion was a psychological desire on the human brain. When I told "Feathers" about my dissertation he immediately offered his services and arranged a series of special private tuition sessions where he was able to work through the theoretical side with me.

I must admit, it was a strange feeling to see my teacher talking me through the sexual themes of *The Good Life*. I mean, this was Mr Featherstone - he was far too much of a gentleman to know about sex! Yet his help in organising my dissertation was absolutely vital to its development and meant that I had the bare bones to flesh out in the coming months. Feathers has always been so methodical in his teaching style and realises the importance of being absolutely clear and concise. With this understanding I was ready to make a start on the research. It was so great to have this time to be able to examine the relationships between some of Britain's finest sitcom characters and establish whether their personal attitudes towards sex actually had a bearing on the success of the shows. The best example of this was the marriage of Basil and Sybil Fawlty, where a lack of intimacy had led to a build-up of angst in both of them. It could be argued that Basil's impotence was a catalyst to the breakdown in their relationship.

Likewise, Alf Garnett in *Till Death Us Do Part* could have suffered from a lack of sexual appetite following the birth of his daughter Rita. His long-suffering wife Elsie showed signs of the mental complaint, which Freud referred to as *Housewife Psychosis:* the hysteria which is attributed to being emotionally and mentally tied to a household and normally having fantasies about cutting loose and being free. I found it fascinating that a two hundred year old thesis could be so relevant to a show written just half a century ago. Every day I would discover another link between Freud and sitcom, whether it was the open relationship between Tom and Barbara in *The Good Life* or the sexual lust of Arkwright in *Open All Hours,* I just loved this feeling of discovery. It was a labour of love for the best part of six months and I was so pleased to get a good mark. To be awarded my honours for my degree, doing something I loved, was just amazing!

This was definitely the feeling I got when I decided to write a biographical drama surrounding the life and work of the legendary Bill Cotton. I knew this was going to take a lot of research and would really push me to the limits of my writing capabilities. But help was on hand. My Uni assistant Joe had been a detective sergeant in the Manchester constabulary and had a hand in the Harold Shipman case. Over the course of the project, Joe was able to teach me the art of thorough research which was absolutely fascinating. It was obvious that in him, I had found a kindred spirit

I was just enthralled by the Bill Cotton era and how one man could have such a dominant influence over the course of television for so many years. How can one man be responsible for so many iconic stars? What was his motivation? Where did he get his foresight from? I didn't yet have the answers to these questions but it was going to be amazing to find them out!

Such a project was a brand-new experience for me. By this time I had built up a substantial repertoire of scripts but they were all based on fictional events and characters from within my mind. Suddenly, I was asking myself to transform a story, which I thought I knew well, into a film script surrounding one of the most influential figures in public service broadcasting. Moreover, tragically he had only passed away a mere eighteen months previously and the entertainment world was still mourning the death of possibly one of the most significant faces behind the camera. So, how the hell did I go about it?

This was something very new to me and although I had researched a lot about this era for my pleasure, I had never been able to devote the time and energy to what I thought this story needed. Being at Uni, I was automatically eligible to take advantage of assets which wouldn't have been open to me if I was doing it independently of education. I just loved the feeling of knowing that whilst I could say I was doing a Master's degree, it opened a lot of doors that would have otherwise remained shut... This included being able to access an endless list of resources and for this bit of research I relied on the celebrity website "Who's Who". If you're not familiar with "Who's Who" it's like a stalker's paradise because it contains the contact information of almost every high profile public figure in Britain. I remember spending hours and hours typing in the names of random celebrities to see if they had made the cut… I was in my element!

So, with my membership to Who's Who assured, I went about obtaining details of significant figures within Bill Cotton's life and career. This is definitely up there with the most enjoyable tasks I have ever done. Joe and I must have scoured the whole site seeing who we could contact, even if it was totally irrelevant to Bill Cotton! After sending out a shed load of letters to stars from the era, I began to lose faith that I would be able to talk to anyone first-hand about the great man. However, one Monday afternoon my mobile phone rang and I asked my assistant John to answer it. It was from Barry Cryer's agent informing me that Mr Cryer (or Baz as he referred to him!) would call me at ten the next morning for an interview about his friend Bill Cotton. I was going to speak to a comedy legend!

To me, Barry Cryer is the pinnacle of entertainment royalty and the thought that I would be speaking to him was beyond comprehension. This was Barry Cryer, a comedy legend - he surely had better things to do than talk to me! Yet he was willing and I for one wasn't going to decline such an amazing opportunity.

When he rang, I discovered fortune wasn't done with me yet. The great Barry Cryer was actually coming to Bournemouth in the same week to take his one-man show to a local theatre. To my amazement he invited me backstage on the night to meet him. Unfortunately, he stated that he wouldn't have time to speak face to face about Bill then, but was more than happy to speak on the phone now. I can still remember the feeling I had for those 30 minutes when I was talking to one of my all-time heroes, it was just indescribable. A bit like a Sunday League footballer chatting to Bobby Charlton, stuff like that doesn't happen.

At the end of the interview Barry reiterated his invitation for me to come backstage to meet him on the Friday night which was the chocolate icing on a three-tier cake. I was absolutely loving this project and it kept getting better. Barry Cryer is definitely an exception to the saying "don't meet your idols" because he is genuinely a lovely man and made that night so special for me. What a star!

With Barry's interview in the bag, it made me hungry to find another comedy God who was willing to speak to me, so you can imagine my delight when I got two comedy legends in one. Ray Galton and Alan Simpson wrote some of Britain's best loved sitcoms of the fifties and sixties, starting with the radio comedy Hancock's Half Hour, before seeing it successfully transfer to television. Not content with one comedy classic, the writing duo then created probably the most bittersweet relationship in British sitcom history;

Steptoe and Son. When the telephone call was arranged, I remember clearly stating the project I was writing. However, minutes into the conversation I quickly realised that their knowledge of Bill Cotton and his work were rather basic. But did this matter? Not one jot! Because I was interviewing two icons of British comedy.

I had to pinch myself. I was suddenly receiving email correspondence from some of the most prolific figures of the twentieth century and irrespective of their response to an interview, I just couldn't believe who was in my email inbox. It was like I was in some sort of dream. Every night I'd ring Mum and Dad and tell them who I'd heard from that day. They were just so happy that I'd found something that I absolutely loved. Such a different experience from my early days of university.

The phone interviews were beginning to pile up. I suddenly found myself speaking to a whole host of influential figures within the world of Light Entertainment, including former controller of BBC One, Sir Paul Fox, the late radio and television presenter, David Jacobs and producer of The Two Ronnies and The Young Ones, Paul Jackson. Phone conversations aren't great for me as I need to get someone to do all the talking and the interviewee doesn't actually get an idea who they are talking to. I imagine they feel a little bit confused because they've arranged to talk to Josh Barry but it's not actually Josh Barry they are talking to. If I was to stop and think about this process, I expect it would frustrate me greatly, but I have accepted that it's a vital technique to help me get to where I wish to be and if it means I have to have a third-party conversation, I'm happy to do it. Despite this, it was here I realised that the art of interviewing was something that I enjoyed immensely and even though not being able to verbally conduct the interviews myself, I still thrived on the art of preparation.

These interviews were all overseen by my cross-platform tutor, Jo Tyler who understood the obvious challenges with me attempting to conduct a telephone interview. She allowed me to use a radio studio where the conversation was beamed all around the room on surround sound. This made it easier for me to interject with follow-up questions as and when I thought of them. For a brief moment I felt like Michael Parkinson and I loved it! This was definitely the area which I could see myself entering into in the subsequent years.

My "Bill Cotton" screenplay, or to give it its full title: 'Educating Auntie', was able to gain me a substantial grade for my Masters project and indeed went a long way to securing me a merit for the entire course. Despite spending the following year writing further drafts, there doesn't seem to be an appropriate outlet for it in the current televisual climate. As a writer I expect rejection because that's just the process. It goes with the territory and if you're going to get offended every time you receive a rejection letter you may want to rethink your career. Yet I remain extremely hopeful that at some point in the future, "Educating Auntie" will have its long awaited moment of glory.

While undertaking the research for Educating Auntie, I interacted with a whole host of agents in my quest to interview the stars. It was here I realised how enormously protective agents can be over their charges. Some of these partnerships had been cultivated over many decades and you could see that the agents didn't see them as clients, more as an extension of their own family. Indeed, when Bill Cotton was in his heyday at the BBC, the Grade Organisation was the most powerful theatrical agency in Britain and even represented Cotton's father, the bandleader Billy Cotton. So I figured that this was a story of loyalty, failure and triumphs and to my knowledge, one that had never been told… until now!

Anything to do with the history of Light Entertainment has always had the power to inspire and fascinate me in a way that nothing else could. I just find it interesting to study the period that saw the transition of stars from the variety stage to television. Unbeknownst to everyone, those agents and scouts who would go around the theatres in London looking for talent, had the power to determine Britain's first television stars. Everyone knows a lot about the eventual stars but less about the way they were selected for television. This was a project I couldn't wait to get my teeth stuck into.

After researching around the subject, I realised that there was very little written about the story of theatrical agents and their role. I was determined to put that right! Yet through not holding any weight within the industry, I realised I had taken on a mammoth project. This was a story which not only spanned generations but the changing face of how Britain consumed entertainment. It became clear that a screenplay would not be able to do this story the justice it rightly deserved as a consequence of the many people and complex relationships involved. So, I knew that if I desired to take this further I would be required to exit my comfort zone of the screenplay and attempt to write a documentary.

Documentaries are quite unlike fictional screenplays and not just from the obvious perspective that you're dealing with fact instead of fiction. This seems like a relatively basic concept to get your head around but when you've spent four years studying the art of drama, it is really hard to cull one's imagination. For me, this was almost impossible. Whenever I went to write anything, a big part of me just wanted to envelope it in a nice little story, drawing on my creative juices but in the back of my mind I knew I couldn't! In the succeeding months I read a great deal on the subject and watched a whole bunch of similar documentaries, just to get an idea as to the stylistic features that are common in these programmes. I reckoned this would help me establish my unique take on the story.

In the same manner that I approached my research on the life of Bill Cotton, I went about tracking down some of the survivors of this story. First on my list was Bob Monkhouse's first agent, Dabber Davis. At the ripe old age of 87,

Davis remains as quick-witted as ever, so attempting to interview him over the phone was extremely entertaining. For over forty-five minutes, myself and my carer, Steve sat silently listening to many anecdotes surrounding the stars of yesteryear and Davis's opinion on the state of entertainment today.

It was clear that Joe from university had taught me well and it was proving relatively simple to obtain telephone interviews with a plethora of major players within the story; Choreographer Dougie Squires gave me a great insight into the BBC variety shows of the 1960's. Veteran magician David Berglas gave me the benefit of his experience being represented by the Grade Organisation and props expert Bob Warans told me of his memories of BBC Television Centre. As the interviews increased I was encouraged to ponder on the execution of the documentary. Could I actually make it myself?

I was in my late twenties and I felt an enormous sense of unfulfillment. By now I had been out of university for almost five years and I still had nothing to show for it. I craved the feeling of accomplishment. If I just wrote another script and sent it off, I would risk having the same problem as I did with Educating Auntie. Could there be another way around this?

Suddenly I recalled Dick Fiddy and his generous assistance on my dissertation and wondered if he would have any advice for me as to where to take this idea next. I searched through the depths of my email inbox to see whether I still had his contact details and then sent him a lengthy email explaining my idea. To my surprise and delight he instantly replied inviting me to the BFI's Southbank site for a "prep meeting". No words could ever describe my utter elation on receiving that email, I had spent years watching him on TV, had had the thrill of emailing him, but now I was going to meet Dick Fiddy in person!

For someone of his calibre to think that my idea had legs was absolutely incredible. Through my life people have often told me that I'm talented in what I do but I always shrug it off, concluding that they're either biased or just being nice. Yet Dick Fiddy's invitation was the proof I needed to show me that people were able to take me seriously and look beyond my disability.

This left me with a dilemma of who to take with me to translate. I felt this was a massive opportunity for me and one that I wanted to make the most of. Eventually, I decided that Joe from Uni would be the best possible choice and luckily for me he accepted. In hindsight I'm still pondering as to whether this was the best decision as on entering the BFI Joe's face showed how fearful he was about letting me down. Part of me felt guilty for putting him in this situation because Joe is one of those people who can't say no to me and would go to the ends of the earth in order to help me. A true friend.

When we arrived at the BFI I could see that Joe was practically shaking with fear, but it quickly dissipated when we met Dick and realised that any nerves were unfounded. I was very conscious about making a good impression so that Dick was in no doubt that I was a credible media practitioner. I wanted to get across that I needed his assistance with the development of my professional idea, not that I was just happy to be there.

Dick is one of the most down to earth people you could ever meet and immediately puts you at ease with his colourful sense of humour. Unbelievably he told me that he thought I had something unique with my idea and encouraged me to go away and refine the concept to make it more appealing for a broadcaster to hang an anniversary on to it. Unbeknown to either of us, this would be the first of many meetings with Dick and in the coming years, Mr Fiddy would become not just a useful contact but a reliable friend. I would like to think that now Dick values me just like any other professional.

With his support, I was able to think about approaching significant figures to interview. Nephew of Lew and Leslie

Grade, Ian Freeman, built a distinguished career as a television consultant before becoming the treasurer of the Royal Variety Charity (or the Entertainment Artistes' Benevolent Fund as it was previously known). When embarking on this project I had a list of people in my head whom I would have loved to interview and undoubtedly anyone who was related to anyone with the name Grade was definitely worth speaking to.

I arranged to meet Ian at the headquarters of a media company where a friend from university was working. They allowed us to use one of their meeting rooms to hold the interview and my carer, James, was able to fire my Parkinson-styled questions at Ian. He answered them eloquently and precisely, whilst subconsciously finding the perfect balance between passion and professionalism. It was obvious that here was a man who knew exactly what he was doing and I just hoped he thought the same about me (I highly doubt it!).

Over the space of an hour, Ian entertained us with tales from his extensive career working as a junior theatrical agent in one of the biggest agencies in the world. I truly felt like a media professional and just loved the buzz that it gave me. I had actually started making a documentary and it felt so good. I just hoped that all of my interviewees would be as obliging as Ian!

Luckily I didn't have long to wait for my second face to face interview, as just one week later I found myself at the Union Chapel in Islington, for an interview with musical director Mike Dixon. In a career spanning over thirty-five years, Mike Dixon has worked alongside some of Britain's best loved stars including Dame Shirley Bassey, Cilla Black and Jimmy Tarbuck to name but a few. We met up with him straight after a matinee performance of Mrs Henderson Presents… which he was providing the music for. Yet on our arrival Mike realised that it is Union Chapel policy for the theatre to lock all its doors following each performance, meaning that we were forced to conduct the interview on a park bench with the backdrop of a busy London road. Not exactly the perfect environment for a radio interview but at least we did get to meet one of the nicest people in show business. Apart from the interview, Mike seemed really interested to get to know me and we soon realised that we had a lot in common. He shares my love for old entertainment shows of yesteryear and it was fascinating hearing him talk about the legends he worked with throughout his career.

On arriving home, I realised that the recording of the interview was not going to be broadcast quality as a result of the traffic noises in the background. Mike and I agreed to re-record the interview in Hammersmith where he was leading a musical masterclass. It was so good to meet him again and instantly he put me at ease. It really was like meeting an old friend. This time the interview sound was a success and we parted having completed a fantastic interview in broadcast quality. I was beginning to really like the documentary making business.

As I said, from the moment we met, Mike and I realised we had a lot in common. He understood that apart from the obvious I was just a normal guy attempting to make a career for myself. Like all the important people in my life, Mike got on board with my hopes and aspirations as our friendship blossomed. To say I'm friends with one of Britain's leading musicals directors is a lovely feeling and I'm sure that me and Mike shall be friends for life.

The next interviewee was to be Mark Fox, the manager of the London Palladium whom I had met several months prior when on a guided tour of that most famous of theatres. I arranged an interview, was really looking forward to it and thanking my lucky stars for such a break when I received an email from a broadcasting legend.

Brian Tesler began his career in entertainment as a producer on BBC variety shows of the early fifties before becoming executive producer of ITV's flagship, Sunday Night at the London Palladium. To me this was entertainment royalty, so I couldn't believe this additional slice of luck! Before the week was out the comedy writer Colin Edmonds, a great friend of Bob Monkhouse and his agent Peter Prichard, agreed to meet me too. I would have three major contributors to the story in one day, extraordinary! On the scheduled date, Mark Fox had been up since the early hours clearing out the store cupboard at the London Palladium. Dressed in old clothes and looking very tired, he'd already done a full day's work and it wasn't even lunchtime! Mark looked like he needed a lie down, so what better way to relax than to be interrogated by me. It was my aim to get his insight into the life of Val Parnell, who was arguably the Palladium's most celebrated manager. It was clear that Mark was not only a theatre manager but a variety historian and just the person to explain about the glory days of Sunday Night at the London Palladium. As a consequence of this, he was able to fill in a lot of missing gaps in the story which I believe gave the documentary a richer texture.

Next up was a big one: the legendary Brian Tesler. Ever since my fascination with television began, Brian Tesler had been a familiar name in my head as a result of his huge dominance within sixties and seventies Light Entertainment. As I grew older and ever more passionate about the business, I became increasingly familiar with Tesler's work, most notably his long and successful relationship with Bill Cotton. To think that I was now interviewing the man himself was just incredible. When he entered the room I could hardly speak and was forced to let James take the lead. All I kept thinking was, "that's Brian Tesler!" and, "I'm sat across the table from Brian Tesler!" Over the next hour I sat engrossed as I listened to tales of some of the biggest stars of British television history as the great man spoke fondly of his early years as a producer. It was obvious that here was a man who loved what he did and boy did it show!

Completing the trio was the celebrated comedy writer Colin Edmonds, who predominantly wrote material for various Bob Monkhouse game shows of the seventies and eighties. A great friend to one of the protagonists of the documentary Peter Prichard, Colin was able to offer me a personal account of what it was like to know, love and work with one of the most successful theatrical agents of all time. It didn't take long for me to realise that Mr Edmonds was a walking talking encyclopaedia on Light Entertainment and I was definitely going to make the most of being in the presence of such an authority on the subject.

With my interviews piling up nicely, I was encouraged to start thinking of other aspects of the production. Firstly, I had to think about a name. For this I relied on the support from Dick Fiddy who sent me his own synopsis of my documentary with the heading ‘Following The Money’. Yet again Dick had hit the nail on the head and I was really drawn to the name, so ‘Following The Money’ stuck! This was brand new territory for me as I had to take charge of every facet of bringing the documentary to life. It felt so good knowing that I could make all the decisions and everyone respected that. First on my agenda was to find a narrator. I knew it would be a hard task as I was adamant on the style and tone of the piece and it would be hard to convey my feelings for the story to a stranger. After researching narrators and voiceover artists, I decided to sign up with an agency who regularly emailed me details of actors looking for work. The idea was that they would contact you if they were interested in your concept. At this point you would send them an extract for them to perform and they would return a sound bite.

For various reasons, each sound bite I was sent somehow didn't match my expectations of how the documentary should sound. Bizarrely it sounded like all of them thought they were narrating an episode of “Rainbow” and I was just waiting for Zippy and Bungle to make an appearance. I was forced to explore other avenues and my former tutor John Foster knew just the man. Actor Russell Biles had grown up in variety, working in a whole range of different theatres on the south coast and had worked with the likes of Tommy

Trinder, Roy Hudd and Roy Castle. I felt this gave him more of an edge over the story he was telling as he had an emotional attachment to the piece. When we met for the first time, I instantly knew Russell would be the perfect person to voice the project, partly because of his knowledge of the subject but mainly because he has one of those voices that you can listen to all day long.

My luck was yet to run out and when my former radio tutor, Jo Tyler offered her services to produce the narration, I almost bit her hand off. Jo and Russell had worked together many times and developed a mutual admiration for each other's work. This made it very easy to work alongside both of them because there was always a relaxed fun-loving atmosphere surrounding them and it was extremely infectious. Jo Tyler remains one of the most generous and patient people I have ever met and her enthusiasm and support throughout the years has been invaluable to my evolution as a writer. It's refreshing to meet a figure in your life who is so selfless and would do anything to see you shine. Irrespective of what I do in my career or where life takes me, I will always remain grateful for Jo's involvement in what I hope is the early stages of my life in entertainment.

If you ever want to send someone round the bend, you should put them in a recording studio for a couple of days and get them to read a seventy-eight page script, before correcting them on their precise pronunciation after every sentence! It's enough to make anyone need to see a doctor. Yet that is exactly what we did to poor Russell. I say poor Russell, he would regularly swear at me and blame me for writing a load of shit that he couldn't say. But, as I always jokingly argued, if he was a professional actor like he's always banging on about, he should have been able to do this with his eyes shut! The first day started well and Russell slowly got into a nice steady rhythm. It was here that I truly realised the painstaking work that goes into radio broadcasting and I was in awe of both of them. Jo instantly knew if Russell had made a mistake without even having to look at him, it was like witchcraft but I knew whatever it was, I loved it. (Even if he was barking mad)!

Over two sessions Russell and Jo were able to work perfectly together to create a narration track to industry standard.

When Jo sent me the final cut, it was so professional, I listened to it and I could hardly believe that I had written and (sort of) directed it. Russell and Jo made it their mission to allow me the creative freedom to direct the piece in the way I wanted. This was a first for both me and Russell so there was a heavy reliance on Jo to tell us if it was up to scratch. In a career spanning over thirty years as a voice artist, Russell had never voiced a documentary on this scale and so was extremely nervous. This nervous energy had a negative effect on his stomach and often he was forced to stop for a banana in the hope that it would silence his noisy belly… luckily it worked!

I left the radio studio feeling extremely buoyant. Not only because I had just made a narration track and was one step closer to a finished documentary, but I had just made a fantastic friend in Russell (but don't tell him I said that)! He is among a very small number of people who was able to look beyond my disability without even knowing me. For some unknown reason we both hit it off from the beginning and now enjoy a love-hate relationship. It is not uncommon for us to have a banterous verbal battle on Facebook Messenger, which I always look forward to. I am sure that Russell is now a friend for life.

The narration sessions were over six months apart meaning that I was required to record all of the remaining interviews during this time. Comedy historian and writer Graham McCann has written a substantial body of work about the beginnings of British Light Entertainment and so I figured he was the perfect person to give the documentary some academic weight. I met him in a seminar room at Cambridge University where I truly realised that I was in the presence of a massive authority on British Light Entertainment. He seemed to know absolutely everything which helped to make the documentary more rounded and insightful.

For my next interview, I looked a little closer to home (yes they do have celebrities on the Isle of Wight!). Broadcaster and journalist John Hannam has been researching and writing about the entertainment business since 1975 when he wrote showbiz related articles for the Isle of Wight Evening Post. During that time, the Island became host to Summer Season shows starring some of Britain's best loved entertainers and John was in the perfect setting to interview them. Today John probably owns one of the biggest interview archives in Britain and the great and the good are queuing up to appear on his radio show "John Hannam Meets…"

John kindly agreed to an interview at my house where he recounted tales about some of the most prolific figures of the twentieth century. It was clear to both of us that we had a lot in common and more importantly, I had found a wonderful resource for celebrity insights. Meeting John for the first time was a revelation. He's an impeccable communicator who remains far more interested in other people rather than himself. Of course this is ironic because John has met and interviewed some of the biggest names in entertainment but still remains so humble about his own life. For over two hours I sat in my kitchen engrossed in tales about Bruce Forsyth, June Whitfield and Tommy Cooper, amongst many more.

I was fascinated by the way John had gone about cultivating a career for himself doing what he loved. Could I do the same?

The project was almost reaching a natural climax and I felt I wanted to mark the occasion in some way. With John Hannam now on board I realised that I had a very important ally and wanted to make the most of it. Initially I had toyed with the idea of creating an interactive exhibition after spending a day at the Grand Order of Water Rats museum in London, looking at the various showbiz artefacts on display. Yet I soon realised just how much content would be needed to fill a room. So I was forced to have a rethink. I finally decided on a launch event where I would play selected excerpts of the documentary interspersed with insightful discussion from a panel of experts in the field.

With this idea in my head I was determined to try and make it a reality. I approached John Hannam to see if he would be interested in presenting the evening and was extremely honoured when he accepted. All I needed was an illustrious panel and I knew exactly who I wanted. Dick Fiddy had been hugely influential in the development of the project and I felt it wouldn't have been right if he wasn't present on a night like this. The undisputed king of the musical baton, Mike Dixon who worked with some of the icons of entertainment so has firsthand experience of stars and their agents, would be invaluable. Finally, Colin Edmonds, whose knowledge of the story is so comprehensive that he could speak on any given subject with authority and grace.

Suddenly I felt like I was back to the days of my cardboard boxes and plastic figures, the only difference being that this was reality. I didn't tell him at the time, but I recall having allocated a figure that resembled Dick Fiddy; if my memory serves me correctly Bubba-Rae Dudley from WWF! (Sorry Dick, I was young and didn't know any better!) But here I was organising a show and everything and everyone were real.

Before I could fully concentrate on the documentary launch, I had one final interview to conduct. This had been a long time coming, almost two years to be precise. During the summer of 2014 one of my best friends tied the knot and for the stag night approximately fifteen of us descended on Cardiff for a night of booze, burgers and boobs. Not getting back to the hotel until 5am, myself and my helper Will passed out on the bed only to be woken up by the sound of my phone ringing at 9am. Surmising that it would only be my mum ringing to check if we were still alive, I told Will to get rid of her as soon as possible. When Will answered the phone, it automatically turned the speaker phone function on and a familiar voice echoed round the room "Hello, this is Jimmy Tarbuck!" For a moment I thought I was still drunk! Jimmy Tarbuck doesn't just ring you up on your mobile does he? Will quickly explained our predicament and asked if we could reconvene at a time when I wasn't half-cut in a cheap hotel room. Probably one of the most bizarre situations of my life but it did provide lively conversation over breakfast.

So it was, that almost two years later, I found myself on the Isle of Wight ferry preparing to meet one of my idols who was appearing alongside fellow entertainment icon, Des O'Connor at the Mayflower Theatre Southampton. I had been instructed by Jimmy to make myself known to the staff at the stage door whereupon they would lead us to his dressing room where we would do the interview. You would think this was simple until James pressed on the intercom buzzer and we slowly discovered that Jimmy had failed to notify any of his entourage that I was coming. Eventually the doors opened (this is where it gets slightly surreal!) to reveal a theatre operative standing with legendary agent Laurie Mansfield's son Peter. After several minutes of explaining, Peter Mansfield suddenly turned to me and said, "Are you Josh Barry?" For a brief moment I felt like a celebrity, Peter Mansfield knew my name!

Our conversation was cut short by a familiar voice coming from another room summoning Peter. James and I listened intently to decipher the conversation between Peter and Mr Tarbuck. A short while later Peter returned with the good news that Jimmy had just agreed to do the interview there and then. Peter escorted us to Jimmy's dressing room where he was so pleased to see me and told James to fire away with my questions. Over the next ten minutes Jimmy Tarbuck gave me one of the best interviews I've ever had the pleasure to conduct. He regaled me with tales of his former agent Peter Prichard, Cilla Black, The Two Ronnies and many more. I was so thrilled to be in the presence of a comedy God.

If I could have told my nine year old self that in just two decades I would be interviewing the great Jimmy Tarbuck, I think he would have laughed in my face. Yet that's exactly what I was doing and no matter what I do in my career I will always be able to say that I've interviewed Jimmy Tarbuck and that's a phenomenal feeling!

Sometimes I wonder if these opportunities would still be open to me if I wasn't disabled. Would people still give me the time? In this respect I guess I'm lucky to be in a fortunate situation where people feel compelled to say yes to me. One of the few bonuses of being disabled.

After the Tarbuck interview we made our way to our seats knowing the documentary footage was complete. And what better way to celebrate than to watch a legend of British comedy doing what he did best. Even at the age of 76, Tarbuck remained as sharp and witty as ever, immediately putting the audience at ease with his familiar style of humour. Without a doubt you could see that he still thrived on the reactions of a live audience. Jimmy and Des entertained a packed-out theatre for over two hours with good old fashioned Light Entertainment which gave me even more reason to believe that there was still an audience who would care about the subject of my documentary.

The recordings were complete but disaster was about to strike as the day after the interview with Jimmy, my proposed editor got called away to work overseas. What was I to do? Without an edited documentary how could there be a documentary launch? Then I recalled an old acquaintance who I'd made during my brief involvement with an amateur dramatics theatre and who was now a part-time DJ and lead singer of a successful local band, Cornerstone. Luckily he accepted the offer to become my editor and it seemed that I would actually have something to exhibit at my launch.

The 17th June 2016 was one of the best nights of my life. It seemed that everything had come together and all I had to do was sit back and watch John Hannam and guests entertain a room full of people. The feeling that the whole evening was solely down to my efforts was something that gave me an indescribable feeling of satisfaction. As I sat and watched the panel wax lyrical about the major themes within the story, I was immediately taken back to my cardboard boxes and plastic figures. Who would have ever thought that all those years later I would be here watching a documentary launch which I had created?

It was then that I realised I had actually been waiting all my life for this moment. No graduations, no special birthdays could ever top this feeling (I feel a Lionel Richie song coming on). Finally I wasn't Josh Barry with Cerebral Palsy I was actually Josh Barry, the media professional. Since embarking upon the project, to date I have had two newspaper articles written about me, one magazine article, one radio show and one blog article. Not bad for someone who cannot be easily understood.

Through university many people used to say, "What a fantastic achievement!" But for me it was just something I did. This however, was the first time I truly felt proud of something I'd accomplished and at that moment I could have taken on the world!

Who knows what the future holds for me but it is reassuring to know that if I continue to meet such generous and loving people then there is no reason why my career can't go from strength to strength. I can't wait to see what's next.

V

Beyond The Stars

Just to clarify, this chapter has absolutely nothing to do with astronomy, before you start thinking I have a worrying fascination with the late Sir Patrick Moore! I thought it would only be right to tell you what I'm up to now (well, "now" as in early 2018. If you're reading this anytime later than 2029 there's a good chance that I'll be in a bed somewhere on the Isle of Wight constantly watching old episodes of Parkinson on a loop for eternity!). Yet you're probably wondering what I actually do with myself now, and believe me you're not alone... Mum and Dad are constantly asking me the same question! Well, I hope this chapter is the perfect answer.

Being a writer is a strange thing because you spend hours and hours creating, devising and writing projects which you think are original and innovative, only to finish them and then start the gruelling process of finding someone who is willing to give you an opportunity. I'd come to the conclusion that it wasn't my time yet and while I could get frustrated by my ongoing sense of unfulfillment, what would that really achieve? I was desperate for that seal of approval which would validate the work I'd been doing for the past seven years. Finally I had a taste of it with the launch of "Following The Money" but at that stage that was all it was, a mere taste. Nothing concrete. I was still yet to find something that would really propel my career in a positive direction.

I'm not one of those people who could lay on the sofa all day watching daytime television. I am a thirty year old freelance writer with endless opportunities at my fingertips and I want to explore all of them. Just because I'm disabled it shouldn't affect my drive and determination to conquer new challenges and horizons.

I really had so much hope that my radio documentary, "Following The Money" would gain momentum and get noticed by the right people but just like my Bill Cotton screenplay, there doesn't seem to be the appetite for that sort of thing in the current entertainment climate. But "Following The Money" wasn't a complete waste of time because it made me stop and think about the world of interviewing in a brand new way. I realised that I got a lot of pleasure in knowing that significant figures within entertainment were answering questions which I had composed. I just loved seeing their initial reaction when they realised the subjects I was bringing up. I'm by no means a journalist but the power to glean insight from someone is something which fills me with joy.

Suddenly it occurred to me that I was surrounded by people who had made a successful career out of interacting with others; Dick Fiddy at the BFI could make addressing a panel of experts on a stage look effortless and as for John Hannam on the Isle of Wight, he's recorded the changing face of entertainment through an extensive catalogue spanning four decades. Scripts and books come and go, people might like them but it's difficult to reveal anything other than what the actual subject is, there's no room for capturing the essence of people. But with interviews, they're a natural timestamp for how people spoke and thought at a particular time in their life. To me it is fascinating to know that I have a growing selection of audio podcasts with some of the most significant figures within entertainment, who all have given me their perception of where they see themselves at that precise moment in time.

John Hannam was a fantastic source of inspiration to me in the conceptual stage of my interviews. For over forty years, he's managed to attract a high calibre of famous people who join him on his Sunday lunchtime show on Isle of Wight Radio. Yet in recent years, embracing new technologies and platforms, he's solely been online in a weekly podcast available for download. You would think this would have been a backwards step for a popular radio slot but it has actually introduced John to a brand new audience and now millions of people from around the world can interact with John and his show. This got me thinking; could I make an entertainment based interview platform for the 21st century? Well, the jury's still out on that one but I could at least give it a try!

For someone who finds it difficult to make themselves understood to new audiences, I recognised the obvious hurdle to me having my own podcast series. I established the name Beyond The Title as a signature for everything I did hence forth and thought it would be great if my website was called the same name. So there it was, Beyond The Title was born

You may be thinking that a podcast series isn't exactly fantastic for someone who isn't easily understood... and you're right! Despite Beyond The Title being my sole creation, you never hear my voice on any of the interviews. This is sometimes the source of my frustration as in my head I sound like a normal human but when I open my mouth the voice of a drunk Sylvester Stallone pops out! Yet if I can convey to my subject that I have done the research myself, written their introduction and composed the questions, then hopefully they will take me seriously.

When I tell people that I'm from the Isle of Wight they normally respond with, "Have you got electricity yet?" or even worse, "Are you inbred?" (It could be an easy explanation for my disability, couldn't it?!). Yet the Isle of Wight surprisingly enjoys quite a vibrant entertainment scene and the two main theatres regularly host the most southerly legs of UK tours for some of Britain's best loved entertainers. Ideal for local journalists to get interviews with the great and good of showbiz. This is exactly how John Hannam started - in fact he refers to himself as a "Stagedoor Johnny." Well, I'm not comfortable with the blatant connotation of that title but I hope you know what I'm getting at!

So I was ready to mix with the stars and all I needed was my first victim/subject. By this time, I was very comfortable with contacting agents and negotiating times and dates in light of "Following The Money". It came naturally to me as I'd been doing it for the best part of six years, but now I'd expanded my pool of potential interviewees to just about anyone and everyone. The prospect of coming in to contact with a whole range of different people encouraged me to once again reflect upon how others saw me. Somehow this felt much more important than worrying about how people interacted with me in a pub or at uni. My subjects may have exactly the same preconceptions as other strangers and as a professional I feel I need to work extra hard to eradicate any wrong beliefs on their part. My aim for every interview is to get an accurate representation of my subject and in turn make them realise that beyond my disability, I'm a fellow professional. Ultimately, my work is Beyond The Title, not Make a Wish foundation!

beyondthetitlle.co.uk launched on the 1st October 2016 with my first guest, the comedian Miles Jupp who'd been on tour with his recent stand up show. Prior to this I'd tried to get comics Paul Foot and Bobby Davro but my terrible organisational skills let me down. Yeah, I'm good at the writing malarkey but absolutely shit at the organisation - I'd be late to my own funeral. So Mr Jupp became the first subject of many interviews made by Beyond The Title and the fact that he was a comic made it all the more in keeping with what I wanted to do.

This was my first opportunity to test out my concept. I still had no idea if this interview style would work, I'd never done anything like this before and suddenly I would be face to face with a household name just hoping that he could answer my questions. I felt an enormous sense of responsibility to get it right. What if Miles Jupp didn't get me? I definitely didn't want him feeling sorry for me or thinking I was some sort of disabled groupie!

When we arrived at the theatre I realised that it wasn't going to be anything like I imagined. When a performer is on tour, every minute is precious as you're on an incredibly tight schedule. For this reason while he was talking to us, he was eating a Chinese takeaway... and he never even offered us a spring roll! Jupp remained extremely relaxed throughout the whole interview and was even interested to know a little more about me and what I did - he'd even heard about Following The Money. It was clear that I wasn't the only one who had done their research! Suddenly I wasn't just an avid, inquisitive fan but a fellow entertainment professional.

On returning home, James downloaded the interview onto my computer and played it back to me. As I sat intensely listening I couldn't believe that I'd actually created a podcast and despite not having the style of my hero Michael Parkinson, I thought we'd done a great job. I just loved knowing that I was responsible for asking questions and the interview was completely controlled by me. I couldn't wait to have this feeling again!

I don't pretend to be the best writer or interviewer - in fact I sometimes think that James has far more talent in asking the questions than I do writing them (but don't tell him I said that!). Yet I attempt to make every interview different from the last and attempt to steer away from obvious questions that they've probably answered a million times. That would make it boring for me, my subject and my listeners. I think it's so boring when you listen to a generic interview with someone where the interviewer has obviously been handed the questions by some work-shy researcher, what is the point? It's so rewarding when they utter the phrase, "Good question, I've never been asked that before." That's when I get an immense sense of achievement and satisfaction in my work - to me, that's what it's all about! I'm not trying to emulate Sir Michael Parkinson but if you're told that you're good at what you do, it's a wonderful feeling. Of course, in some cases they could just be being patronising thinking, "Oh look, isn't it sweet that the disabled guy wants to ask me some questions!" But I try not to think about it like that - every little helps!

Like Miles Jupp, most figures I meet understand that I am just a fellow media professional. No greater example of this was when I met the celebrated television writer Tony Jordan who immediately treated me as an equal. My background in scriptwriting greatly interested him. Usually, after the interview my subjects make their excuses and leave but Tony was so fascinated by the way I worked that we were able to enjoy a substantial chat afterwards. We chatted about everything from getting my first break to the purpose of university but above all, he was talking to me, not the people around me. I was being taken seriously and it felt great!

Up until this stage, apart from my obvious physical requirements, my disability had never been an obstacle to my reaching out to people. I was adamant that the two were mutually exclusive. Indeed, I realised that by being a minority myself it could give me a window into a world which I hadn't imagined. Despite me being adamant not to allow my disability to limit my career, I realised that as an interviewer, people are required to put their trust in me in order to tell their story. This is easier when we are able to find a middle ground to form the basis of an understanding. So when encountering someone who has had to go through similar obstacles in order to gain success, I think we both see something in each other which will benefit both of our professional careers. When the actress Leslie Ash received an interview request from 'Beyond The Title' she was very interested to meet me. Not because she'd heard about my impeccable interviewing skills (though that's a concrete fact!) but because I was a fellow disabled person in the Arts. When we eventually met it was obvious that she felt great empathy with me and my plight because she was going through similar situations. I was totally in shock as Leslie gave us an insight into life after her medical treatment and the discrimination she faced within her own industry - I was utterly gobsmacked! How could a hi-profile actress such as Leslie Ash be the subject of prejudice just because of her disability? It's utter madness and let's hope things can change in the coming years so that people like Leslie can continue to shine.

If Leslie Ash was struggling with her disabled identity, then Paralympic legend Dame Tani Grey-Thompson had already fully conquered it. The most decorated Paralympian in history swapped the racing track for Westminster in 2010 when she became invested into the House of Lords and now tackles issues facing disabled people in twenty-first century Britain. Myself and James got suited and booted and made our way to Westminster. Waiting in the foyer of the House of Lords was one of the most surreal experiences of my life. All I kept thinking was, "What am I doing here?" The foyer was filled with more celebrities than the Channel Five autumn schedule: Noel Edmonds, Robert Winston, Joan Bakewell - I tell you, if it hadn't been so quiet I would have been networking like hell! I would love to meet Joan Bakewell - does that sound a little creepy?

When we got into Tani's office, it became clear that beyond the pomp and ceremony, she is a down to earth person who wants to make disabled people equal in our society. Yet somehow this wasn't the outright disability rights that I absolutely detest. Tani just wants disabled people to be able to go through the same mundane frustrations as everyone else, but with the right access. It was here that I realised that "disabled rights" and inclusion don't always need to be opposite ends of the spectrum and if done right, they can actually work in harmony with each other. Tani is such an intellectual and eloquent individual and I can honestly say that she changed my perception of how I see myself.

Having such meaty interviews with fascinating women, I was slowly starting to realise the full extent of the potential power of my website. Up until this point I had never thought about the legal side of my work and I wanted a bit of consolidation, so I joined the Writer's Guild of Great Britain, (I know I probably should have done it sooner but I've mentioned before that organisation isn't my strong suit!).

One day I was perusing the weekly newsletter from the Writers Guild and noticed that legendary comedy writers Laurence Marks and Maurice Gran, were heading up a seminar at somewhere called, The Museum of Comedy. I thought this was my sort of place and just had to attend! But you know me, I couldn't just attend without enquiring as to the possibility that I could interview the two sitcom giants and when I discovered that their agent was an old acquaintance, Peter Mansfield, Jimmy Tarbuck's agent who had helped me with Following The Money, everything just fell into place.

The Museum of Comedy was everything I hoped it would be and more. Situated in an old underground pub, this theatre is a real tribute to the classic comics of the past. As soon as I stepped foot in the door I knew that I was somewhere very special. Framed photos from iconic comedy shows adorn the walls, complemented by comedy memorabilia all adding to the authenticity of the place and the upcycled church pews give it a spiritual feel. I think you'd agree, an ideal setting to interview two sitcom greats.

For the next twenty minutes, I sat engrossed as Laurence Marks and Maurice Gran waxed lyrical about their unparalleled career in comedy and the many performers they'd worked with over their forty-year tenure. This was a real honour for me as I'd seen all their shows, watched many interesting interviews with them but now I was face to face with these two great men and I felt slightly out of my depth. Marks and Gran are icons of television comedy and to find myself sitting across a table from them with my carer, Ben asking them *my* questions... it was just totally amazing. At that moment I wouldn't have swapped my life with anyone else.

I found it fascinating to hear about the beginnings of Birds of a Feather and how they found Pauline Quirke and Linda Robson to play those parts so effortlessly. And their fondness for their other highly successful shows, Shine On Harvey Moon and Goodnight Sweetheart. I felt like a kid in a sweet shop - which gem should I have next? Inspirational and thought provoking stories are great but personally, nothing can beat unpicking the art of making people laugh. It was utterly fascinating!

When the interview was over, Ben and I hung around waiting to go into the theatre and all of a sudden the legendary Barry Cryer walked through the door. Well, I couldn't contain my excitement, I just had to go over and say hello. That was the precise problem, I couldn't find the breath to say hello, it was like my body was eating itself! I was wobbling around like a nodding dog on a rollercoaster! Although I had met him before at a theatre in Bournemouth, this was the first time I'd seen him at a social event and there was just no way I was leaving without attempting to request an interview with the great man. To my amazement, Barry replied, "Yes, let's do it." - I couldn't believe it, I was going to interview a comedy icon in person!

For those of you unfamiliar with the work of Barry Cryer (how could you?!), he's a legendary writer and performer who has provided material for some of the greatest comedians of all time, including Morecambe and Wise, Frankie Howerd, The Two Ronnies and Kenny Everett to name but a few. In short, he's been integral to the development of the most iconic comedy shows over the last sixty years. This is everything I'm passionate about and Barry has been integral to all of it. So you can imagine my excitement when James and I arrived at the house of this true comedy giant ready to interview one of my all-time heroes. For over forty five minutes, the great man recounted tales from his remarkable career including the most name drops Beyond The Title has ever heard! Where do I start? Princess Margaret, Rudolph Nureyev, Judy Garland, Bruce Forsyth... I was in a daze, I never thought I'd ever be hearing first-hand accounts of giants of entertainment from another giant. Definitely a tick off my bucket list! If this has got your tastebuds going the interview is still available along with my whole back catalogue on beyondthetitle.co.uk

Now, you'd think that one comedy legend was enough for one week but remember this is me, I don't do anything by halves! So, what's better than one comedy legend? Two comedy legends... and in the immortal words of the late Bruce Forsyth, "You get nothing for a pair," but that's what I did when I arrived at a prestigious golf club to interview the great Jimmy Tarbuck. Maybe sometimes I don't give my helpers enough credit for the assistance they give me in regards to my professional life. I guess part of me wants to do everything myself but I realise I can't. James is really good at helping me develop professional relationships with figures within my industry and Peter Mansfield in particular is someone that James has made sure we keep in touch with. So when I was looking for another comedy legend to appear alongside Barry Cryer, James knew just the person! Peter is someone I'd had contact with since the creation of the Bill Cotton screenplay and has been a useful contact in my plight to research and interviews stars of showbiz. Also, since the sad death of the celebrated agent Peter Prichard, he has been

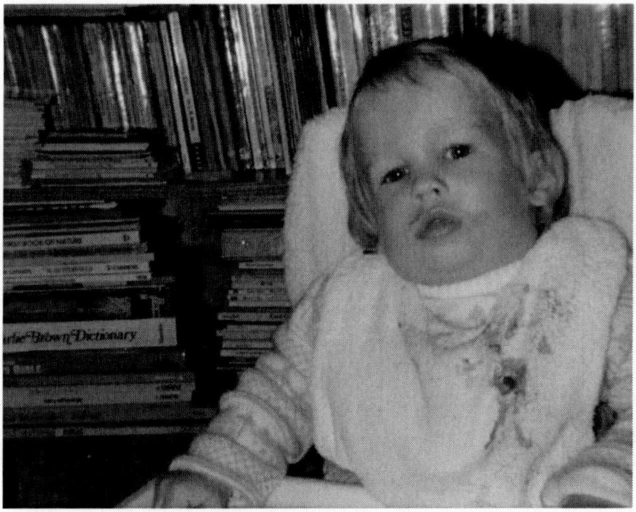

Me Aged 3

With Sophie at our childhood home

Me in my first John Care Chair

Me in the hoist

Me & Di

Me and my friends on a school trip to the Millennium Dome in 2000

With Gramps

With Grandma

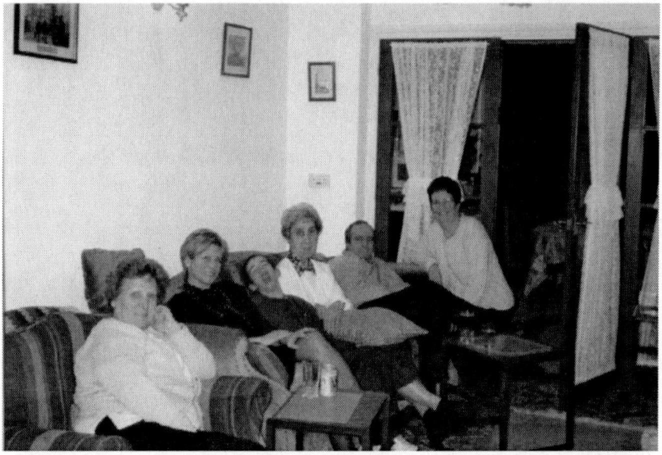

(From left) My Auntie Pat, Mum, me, Aunty Mary, Dad and Aunty Elizabeth

(From left) Di, Beryl, Alice, Penny and Maretta

Me with Calum

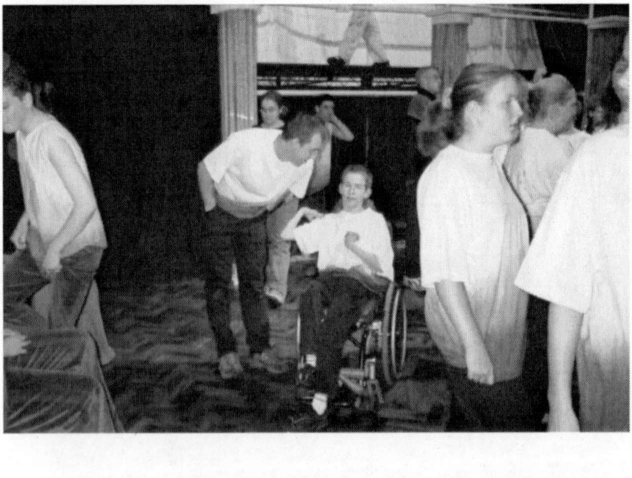

Me and Steve on the set of Jesus Christ Superstar

Me and Harry (left) and Spud (right)

Me and Nick (My carer at Uni)

Me and Sara (top left), Graeme (bottom left) and Roubina (right) friends from University

Me and Tom Kidd (carer in my gap year)

personally responsible for looking after Tarby. So James figured it wouldn't hurt to ask! James phoned Peter and within an instant he said "How about Monday?" Could it be that easy? Although I'd also met Jimmy before, this too, like Barry Cryer's interview, seemed different. Yet again, I was about to do a formal interview with one of my idols!

It's no secret that Jimmy Tarbuck and golf go together like cheese and biscuits, so where else would we meet than the place where he spends the majority of his day? But this was no ordinary golf club. I mean, what other golf club has complimentary aftershave in the toilet?

When we arrived at the reception of the golf club, I overheard two guys telling the receptionist that they were from the BBC, there to do an interview with Jimmy for a documentary about Ken Dodd's 90th birthday. The receptionist then turned to me and my carer Will, asking us the purpose of our visit. It turns out that Jimmy Tarbuck's organisational skills are almost as good as mine as it would appear that he'd double booked himself and was currently halfway through his standard eighteen holes. So for the next three hours me, Will and the BBC crew waited in a big lunch lounge for our subject to return from the sport he loved. Two sets of people waiting for an interview, Tarbuck was a busy lad!

My PA, Will is a stereotypical English gentleman: extra polite, avoids confrontation and becomes extra patient and generous around new people... the complete opposite of me - if I could have made myself understood I would have stated that there would be no way I was being Tarbuck's sloppy seconds. But being the ever-present ying to my yang, Will had already stated that we should allow the BBC to have Jimmy first, but I knew Jimmy wouldn't see it like that. When he arrived on a golfing cart, the men from the BBC strolled out to meet him, obviously hinting that they wouldn't settle until he was in a chair waxing lyrical about his fellow Liverpudlian, Ken Dodd. Jimmy politely shook their hands and made his way over to me and said, "Right chaps, let's do this!" The first and last time I think I'll ever get one over on the BBC!

Although he obviously had limited time, Jimmy Tarbuck was determined to answer all my questions. As I sat and listened to Will deliver them to this showbiz God, I was struck by how effortless Tarbuck was making his responses. It was like he was reeling them off from an internal script but not in a bad way, it was just that here was a man who knew exactly what he wanted to say from years in the spotlight. As someone who finds it difficult to make myself understood, I was totally in awe of his command of the English language. Tarbuck remains a really nice family man who is very philosophical about his many successes. No wonder he has so many people queuing up to be his friend and I for one would love to count Mr Tarbuck amongst my pals.

The interview with Jimmy was the perfect Christmas present to my growing fans on beyondthetitle.co.uk. When you have a big name such as Tarbuck, it expands the interest in what it is you're trying to do. The Jimmy Tarbuck interview remains the most popular interview on my website and gave me my record number of views when it was released three days before Christmas 2017. If I can keep attracting that calibre of person to the Beyond The Title microphone then surely the only way is up.

So being an old romantic, I think this is a perfect place to end this chapter. I have finally found something that I love to get up for each day. It fulfils that thing in me that still believes I could be top of the bill at the London Palladium (of course I wouldn't ever do that unless they were intending to bring back Bill and Ben!). Yet this is where I want to be, doing something that I love. I just can't wait to see who or indeed what's next for Beyond The Title, so make sure you tune in every Friday to beyondthetitle.co.uk to see who I've coerced into my wicked web!

VI

Vegetable Soup

Random chapter heading I know, but I couldn't think of anything else to call a chapter about my identity. Alas, I'm not about to give out my PIN number and if I did you wouldn't get very far... well, it depends how this book goes! But again, I digress. I expect that part of the reason why you bought this book was to get a take on disability by someone who is just that. So by chapter six I bet you're shouting at the pages, "GET ON WITH IT!" So best I do just that!

There's always been something very ordinary about my family, we lived in a two-up, two-down town house, surrounded by neighbours who became integral to our lives. Inside a tight community there was never any need for people to treat me differently. From a very early age my parents were determined that I would be able to live as much of a mainstream life as possible alongside Soph. Despite this, my parents remained open to a whole range of help and advice which was put their way and were willing to learn from others in a bid to enhance the quality of my life. After all, they themselves were learning how to care for and support a child with severe disabilities, they had never done that before. Disability was as alien to them as the people who looked at me differently in the street.

The Isle of Wight is a small place, so if you're disabled you do know everyone else who is disabled. I always find it amusing when people just assume that disabled people know each other, like we're part of some kind of cult (possibly an idea for 'The Avengers' movie spin off?). Yet when you've got a disability on a small island, you do come into contact with others in your situation either trialling new equipment or at charity days out. Indeed, my family support workers Alice and Beryl ran a monthly group called Toy Library where families could congregate and learn from each other about the best ways to support their children. Alice and Beryl ran activities which were inclusive for almost everyone irrespective of ability. It was like any other parent and toddler group, except most children attending had four wheels instead of two legs.

Added to this experience, was playing alongside the children within our estate at home, so I actually had the best of 'both worlds'. I knew what it was like to go to a normal kids' party and used to enjoy getting involved in the activities that I could do. Yet if we attended a party of a child from Toy Library, I would still be able to get involved with everything. For Mum, this wasn't about admitting defeat with the activities I couldn't do, but finding a way around it which meant I could. If you have a bouncy castle and every child can't stand up, it's safer than having just one disabled person getting trodden on.

Alice realised that I had the ability to be very sociable with a whole range of different people. Why couldn't I stop in the street and have a word with Harry the greengrocer? But unfortunately there were not enough hours in the day to give this opportunity to every child. So Alice created Toy Library for parents and children to come and meet together in an informal setting where she could offer advice and support. This was a rare opportunity to meet and witness other people in my situation but it was never clinical or thrust down our throats as Alice was all about family. She understood that in order to help the disabled children she worked with, she would have to understand the dynamics of the families. It was bespoke support at its very best.

Somehow I don't identify myself with other disabled people. It's never been something that I've thought about. Never do I think, "I wish I had someone who was in my situation who I could talk to", to me that seems irrelevant. Everyone is different and when I do get frustrated about stuff I find it's mostly my own attitude towards my limitations, not my limitations themselves. There is no doubt that I have unresolved issues which I need to address about my disability, such as planning for the future, my ongoing frustration between the life I want to live, the life I can live and the people who can help me achieve it and I guess I'm not alone in this. There are a lot of people all over the world with this predicament but I don't honestly think that they would be able to help me or vice versa.

That is not to say that I didn't have opportunities to mix with people who did actually share my disability. I recall when I got my first electric wheelchair, a series of classes were arranged at the local special school, think Top Gear without a racist and sexist bigot, well… I was there so…

This was so much more than wheelchair training. For me it was the first time in my life that I could mix with people who were of a similar condition. Even writing this now I can remember my feelings towards the wheelchair lessons. I didn't object to the lessons themselves but it was just the social situation that we were put in. We didn't know each other from Adam (whoever he was) apart from the occasional "SCOPE fun day" or a "Toy Library" day out, yet we were expected to integrate with each other even though we all had very severe communication issues. This was possibly the first time that the CP sufferers from the class of 1987 had come together in one room (it was a bit like Robot Wars).

Despite my tenderness of years, I remember being faced with a dilemma: did I just sink into the crowd and wait for it to be over? Or did I make myself heard? I guess I became the class clown and when my physio, Marie-Ann, asked me the question, 'What do you do if an old lady crossed the road?' I replied, 'Run her over...' which was received with laughter and amusement from everyone in the room.

Now, I don't want you to get the wrong idea about me and think I'm some sort of disability hating psycho. I'm not. This is no crusade against disability, it's more an explanation of where I am coming from and I am merely expressing that, just because people are born a certain way, does not mean that they should be bound together as a result of having one thing in common. Personally, I don't think disability should be a criteria to base your whole life around. The world is a big place and there are opportunities for everyone irrespective of race, gender or ability, everyone finds their own path in life. Look at Donald Trump!

When it came to thinking about my education, there was never any doubts that I would attend a mainstream school. That attitude was very revolutionary for its time, as even in the early 1990's it was almost unheard of that a physically disabled child should be able to attend a mainstream school. Yet my parents were adamant that I take part in the mainstream educational system and even before the age of two, began to make pathways into local education. After all, I had done everything else that a normal child would do; children's parties, roller skating, I'd even had chicken pox! Why couldn't I go to school? We were lucky enough to have the support of Alice and Beryl who were determined to assist in gaining me inclusion into state education. Yet, as a result of my complex requirements it was realised that it would take time to create devices and techniques which would assist my learning.

The Barry family home was situated within an urban estate, close to the centre of Cowes on the Isle of Wight, which had recently seen the erection of a local primary school. Lauren, my eldest sister, was already enrolled and was looking forward to the prospect of attending a brand new school as the climax to her primary education. It was always assumed that when Soph and I reached the appropriate age, we too would enrol at the same school. After all we had been attending the playgroup twice a week for the best part of a year and had made many friendships which would hopefully develop and flourish throughout our primary education. Due to a variety of reasons, Mum eventually felt that we needed to explore other alternatives and after trekking around and visiting many schools in the area, she came across a village primary school on the outskirts of Cowes, called Northwood Primary. It was led by a young enthusiastic head teacher, Vicky Johnson. My Mum arranged a meeting with Vicky, took me and Soph along and discussed the possibility of the school taking me on. Originally Johnson was led to believe that it was just Sophie who was in need of a place at school and thought it would be possible to squeeze her in for the following academic year, but my Mum replied, 'What about Josh?' This statement stunned Vicky Johnson for a second, but, after a moment of reflection, she suggested that I should wait a year while the school could be adapted to suit my individual requirements and then commence my schooling a year later than my peers. What a result! It finally looked like my parent's hard work and dedication to the cause had finally paid off!

During that year out it was organised that my Mum would educate us from home with the help of Caroline, my playschool helper who, rather than supporting me at school, would support me at home with my Mum. This was a very daunting time for everyone, as it was also to be the first time I would be left alone with someone who was unknown to the family. It was very important that the new appointment was absolutely suitable to my needs. When we appointed Penny, our reservations were put to rest as she fell into the role perfectly. The whole process was overseen by the special educational needs advisor, Kit Hartley who offered the school help and advice in matters of inclusion. It was as a result of the hard work and enthusiasm of Hartley, Di, Vicky Johnson, Alice and Beryl, together with my parents that this dream of mainstream schooling, became a reality.

Even though I started a year later than my peer group, the school had the unique ability to make my disability almost invisible to both staff and students. It offered the same experiences to me as to my able-bodied peers. It also offered the same behaviour standards. Except, when one day the head teacher received a phone call from a disgruntled parent who wished to make a complaint against a child who had been bullying her son. Mrs Johnson asked, 'What is the name of the pupil?' To which the irate parent replied, 'Josh Barry, in Year Four.' Somehow this other kid had pissed me off so much that I had felt the need to ram him with my electric wheelchair. The normal reaction would have been for Mrs Johnson to call me into her office and give me a telling off, but this was not a normal situation. Instead she came down and sang the praises of Penny who had managed to remain so 'invisible' that neither the child in question, nor the parent, had ever taken into consideration my disability. Finally, this was inclusion! (And if you're reading this and you were that boy, I am very sorry and I know I should have got a telling off!).

My time at Northwood Primary School was an altogether happy experience for both me and the extensive team around me. From being the Bethlehem taxi in my first school nativity, to my portrayal of Mr Muller in my leaver's production of the Pied Piper, there was no obstacle too large. As a result, Northwood was able to welcome many more disabled students to its warm and loving nest in the years to come, and create even more success stories of inclusion at its very best. Since my departure from the school, both my Mum and Dad have helped many more disabled children achieve their educational potential within the walls of this very special learning establishment.

Going from the warm-hearted safeness of Northwood Primary School to Middle School didn't only bring educational change but also social. It was here where I got to know Joe, a long term friend with Cerebral Palsy which affects the lower part of his body. The Isle of Wight is a small place so I had come into contact with him before but this was the first time we were able to socialise. A fan of classic television and music it didn't take long for us to realise that we had shared interests. However being in separate classes meant that it was only when we got to High School that we were able to socialise. Never forced or controlled, our relationship was able to grow organically and when I realised that at High School I was going to have to share a work room with him, I was grateful to have a mate alongside me.

Despite shared interests, Joe and I have always been very different. As a fantastic musician, Joe is always far more at home playing to a crowd rather than being in it. Something that I always admire about him, I would love to have the confidence to entertain a big audience but I just can't. I love being in the middle of the action, having a laugh. This situation is very difficult to explain to an outsider as Joe and I realise and respect each other's social requirements and it's never been a problem for us to mix. Just like when I encounter a carer who doesn't understand that I just want to do the things that others do. When either Joe or I have a chaperone on a night out, they automatically assume that we need to be stuck together like Velcro. In any normal situation when you're out with a crowd you don't just talk to one person all night, why should Joe and I be any different? I think that if he was being honest then Joe would tell you that my conversation is very boring.

This attitude has surrounded us for our entire friendship and it's something that we always laugh at now. Why do people think that just because we are disabled friends that we have to be inseparable? It's crazy! People don't think this about any other minority - no one says "My mate has brown eyes, do you know him?" That would be ridiculous but why should people assume that disability is a members' club?

When we got to high school, it was agreed that the disabled students would have a work room in order to carry out activities that they couldn't do in a class room setting and I was so excited when I discovered that I would be working next to Joe. We shared the room with another guy called Todd Venables who was a year older than us and suffered from muscular dystrophy.

I would share the rest of my school years with Joe and we would eventually develop a bond as a result of the close proximity in which we worked. Personally in a perfect world, I would have just liked my own little cubbyhole just for me, Penny and Di, but I guess even cripples need to learn to share!

The idea of separate workstations was greeted by a substantial amount of excitement from the special needs department, who had been campaigning for this to be established for a long time. There seemed to be a bizarre, unexplained euphoria about the development and the decision as to what the room would be called generated great anticipation from all parties involved. Well, apart from yours truly who could not have given two shits! Personally, I wouldn't have cared if it had been named 'Cripples R Us' or 'The Vegetable Soup Room' as I didn't think it was relevant, it was just a work space. Ultimately, the consensus decided that it should be named 'The Den'. A bit of a crap name but I suppose you can't have everything. It sounds more like a level on a "Super Mario" game or what you'd call somewhere you buy drugs.

I was absolutely perplexed as to why everyone saw it as such a treat. I just saw it as a practical space where we could work. Anyway, "The Den" was born and saw me through many turbulent years on my path to adulthood. Apart from the fact that we were disabled, the three boys of "The Den" could not have been more different. Joe and Todd had already made the decision they wanted to work with male helpers and were supported by men of a certain age who differed in their approach towards their charges. Todd had a high level of intelligence and wit in plenty, so he could occasionally out smart and challenge the outlandish behaviour of his helper Dick. It didn't take long for me to realise that Dick and I had the same sense of humour and I made it my mission to attempt to shock him at every given moment. This left Joe, who ironically worked with my former next door neighbour Geoff, who fell in between the fine line of sanity and madness.

So, for the best part of four years our dysfunctional school family lived and worked alongside each other for six hours a day, five days a week in the confines of a 15x12 foot room and shared many happy memories, thus proving to myself that it was possible for me to integrate with other disabled students. I guess I was drawn to Dick's cheeky-chappy personality and found it easy to join in with his gentle jostling. It was like our own community: we'd frequently have 'in jokes' about the teachers or observe bizarre behaviour in fellow pupils. Somehow this atmosphere appealed to me and I felt very comfortable in their company. Yet this feeling came at a price. I realise now that this could have been a fabrication of my own insecurities about my disabled identity. When I was in the Den I loved the banter between myself and Dick and we all got on well, but in the back of my mind I realised that I could have used this time to reinstate myself within a friendship group of likeminded people who were not bound together by their physical limitations. I liked the Den and everyone in it but just thought there was more to my school life than being with the same seven people all the time. This made me feel very paranoid about what others thought of me, that in some way I was thinking that I was better than everyone else… I definitely wasn't! I knew Joe didn't have a problem with this. He is so laid back and chilled out that I doubt he even thought of it, but because school is such a socially conscious environment everyone is always making sure that you're attending everything and you're seen at the right places, just to say you were there. Yet at the end of the day, it's irrelevant, so why does it matter? If people are more comfortable in an intimate situation why would you push them to attend something that they might not enjoy? That's why I hate nightclubs because I haven't got any control over the situation and can see why this social interaction isn't for everyone. I don't think disabled people should feel pressurised into doing something that they're not comfortable with just to fit in with other people. So maybe in this situation, opportunities like "The Den" are a great thing because it's having the best of both worlds, you're still living alongside the mainstream world but with tailored expectations. Maybe if I adopted this philosophy, I wouldn't feel so dissatisfied with my own life.

What a way to end a chapter eh? I think this sums up my lifetime battle with my disabled identity. I hope you don't think I have been slightly harsh in my opinions about disability. Despite being heavily dependent on others, why should I let my disability define me as a human being? I always prefer talking about the latest bit of gossip or taking the piss out of someone, rather than discussing wheelchair components or disabled equipment. However, I think it's more than ok to be either type of person. I just believe that beyond the wheelchair and equipment there is a far more interesting world to explore and I want to make the most of it.

VII

One of the Gang

You may not believe it but I still find it a little ironic that I've actually written this book, because I think my disability has no influence over the course of my life whatsoever. In fact I hate talking about my limitations and consequences of my disability as it's not who I am. They are just physical components of my everyday life, they don't define me. If you're interested, I think what defines who I am is the people that I have surrounded myself with over the years. The people who have accepted and facilitated my belief that I should live as much of a normal life as possible alongside everyone else. At the end of the day I am and have always wanted to be, one of the gang.

Although the last chapter may have been about my struggle with my disabled identity, I don't actually worry about that anymore. Instead I just go about my everyday life as I always have done with the people who know me. Almost everyone who has ever made an impression on me has been able-bodied and like a feral kitten who has been taken in by a pack of dogs, I now consider myself "one of them".

As soon as I could talk, I remember being very determined to communicate with everyone whom I came into contact with. Growing up in a quiet, close knit estate meant that there would always be visitors coming in and out of our house. I saw how Lauren and Soph were so verbal with everyone and thought, "Why can't I have a bit of that. While some in our community were patronising and didn't understand my mental capability (or lack thereof), others made it their mission to interact with me and promptly realised that apart from the obvious, I was just a normal lad. It was at the local working men's club (of course I would have a sip of beer because that's what all young kids do), in a loud environment, that was the first time I had to battle with a lot of background noise and had to work a lot harder to make myself understood. This stood me in good stead for later experiences in a pub setting. The men in that club spoke to me like any other child because they didn't know any different. I was just Josh and that's how I liked it.

As a result of my communication difficulties, it proved a little harder for me to contribute to these social situations if I did not have the presence of a key person, who either knew what I was saying, or knew their way around my communication book. Up until the age of fifteen, a substantial component of my communication relied on an alphabet chart where I would spell words which I wanted to say instead of speaking them. It may have looked like an elaborate fusion between hangman and chess but this system proved to be successful for over a decade and broke down some of the obvious barriers between me and everyone else.

Today I find it ridiculous to think that I had to rely on a book to facilitate 70% of my verbal interaction. I don't know how I kept my patience! If you asked me to conduct a conversation using an alphabet chart today, I expect I would pick it up and throw it at you before I could make a sentence. So, I feel a great sense of empathy for those people who have to rely on a communication aid throughout their life. In retrospect, this communication barrier was yet another hurdle for me to overcome in order to gain social acceptance, especially when my spelling abilities had reached a substantial level beyond my tender age, thus making it very difficult for my peer group to understand and comprehend the words I was spelling out to them. Sometimes it did feel like I was having a third party conversation because an adult would have to stitch the sentence together and relay it back to my mates like Chinese whispers.

Also, my mates understandably lacked the patience to remain interested in the conversation while I tapped my utterances out on my spelling board, which impacted heavily on the art of conversation and my ability to make bonds. Looking back, it was a lot to expect of six year olds to attempt interaction with such an unusual communication method. It was suitably assisted by Penny, who would be able to gauge if a child had problems in understanding me and would be on hand to facilitate whenever needed.

In later years my communication book would prove the subject for amusement, as my lunch time assistant would teach me and my friends how to spell swear words through tapping them out on my alphabet board. This became the most popular activity of our lunch break and sometimes I wouldn't finish my lunch through laughing so much. I just had to make sure during spelling tests, when asked to spell duck, my spastic hand would not find its way to the 'F'! Despite trialling alternative communication aids such as a lightwriter; a small computer with a built in speaker and pre-recorded sentences (which proved successful until Calum thought it would be funny to change the pre-recorded messages to chat up lines, which got a lot of funny looks at school), the communication book proved to be my favoured way of interacting for the best part of a decade and without it my social life may have been dramatically different.

After a triumphant battle with communication, I was ready to integrate myself amongst my peer group. As a result of starting school a year late, after my first year in reception it was agreed that myself and my sister should move up, not just one but two years, in order to catch up with our age group. There was great concern that this may harm our educational progress. Yet the foundation which my Mum had laid during the year in which we were home educated, was vital to our ability to maintain a level of learning which meant we could be on par with our peer group.

Luckily for me, I fell into a friendship circle that was willing to look beyond my disability and ignore the extra baggage which surrounded me. Before long they realised that, apart from the obvious outside appearance, I was just a normal seven-year old with exactly the same desires and interests as them. Therefore throughout our remaining years in primary education myself and the two other boys, Andy and Joe, (not the previously mentioned Joe who has CP) developed a strong relationship and were allowed free rein in the activities we chose to get involved with, irrespective of my disability. Joe had already cultivated a very adult sense of humour which somehow appealed to me. From bog flushing himself at Cubs to asking my part-time female helper Joanne what was meant by shagging, he always had the ability to make me laugh! Andy, or to give him his full title, Andrew Barber, completed our trio. He was a very shy and timid boy who would come out of his shell on very intimate occasions and illustrated that he had a sense of humour which could give mine a run for its money.

Together with these two boys, I was able to forge friendships for the very first time. I was regularly invited around their houses without a parent or a carer. We did everything together; football, Cubs, sleepovers, parties and swimming, I don't remember my disability ever being a factor in what we did, we were just very good friends and whatever they did, so did I. Twenty years on, me and Andy still act like school children with the added benefit of alcohol! We still have the same immature sense of humour and I was very privileged and honoured when he asked me to be the best man at his wedding. This was the ultimate acknowledgement of the regard he held me in and made me feel that I was important. We had been friends for a long time, but there was still a part of me unsure as to what my friends really thought of me. Do they still see me as a charity case? Although I like to hope that people are able to ignore my differences, I remain paranoid as to what they really think and this gesture was enough to maybe dilute those thoughts for a moment.

When it was time to go to middle school, our other friend Joe revealed that he would be starting at the rival school (when I say rival, this wasn't the Bronx, it was Cowes! The closest thing we got to a gang was Kool and the…). So our tightknit group was forced to disperse. This left myself and Andy facing life at middle school without the joker of our pack who always made it easier for people to get to know me. On reflection, this is a dilemma that I have been faced with during every stage of my life. In order for people to become comfortable with me they require a reliable figure to make communication achievable and without such a figure how was I going to integrate?

I bet some of you are still a little confused as to why or even how I made friends with such a "normal" group of people... don't worry, you're not alone! In fact I sometimes struggle to get my head around it. It's not something that you think about and it wasn't until I got to Uni that I realised how unique it was. In certain circumstances people don't have the patience to get to know "different" people, do they? This doesn't have to be limited or attributed to university, in fact it's any social discourse. When people are propositioned with the idea of communicating with someone a little different both parties are worried about remaining patient and being made to feel uncomfortable. Although perhaps it isn't patience. Perhaps it is fear of the unknown?

As part of my research for this book, I interviewed Andy about his experiences of having someone like me as a best friend. I was determined to understand what impact it had on his ability to make other bonds and indeed the reaction of people when he tells them that his best mate has Cerebral Palsy. He said that at first people are taken aback and even make remarks such as, “Isn't that cute,” or “Ah that's so nice of you.” However, when he reveals that it's just like any normal relationship and, when they meet me in person, they become much more accepting and are able to understand why it is that he chooses to be friends with me.

When meeting new people or in a new situation with people who are unknown to me, it is sometimes very difficult to initiate the first move. In my experience, listeners to my speech become both apprehensive and irritated with themselves when it comes to speaking to me. Their preconception leads them to think that I will somehow become both offended and impatient with them if they do not understand my utterances. It’s a funny concept. I mean they don’t think that about French people who speak in broken English do they? Or those lovely people in Bombay call centres! On the contrary, I do not think of it as an issue, irrespective of how many times I am required to repeat myself. If they still struggle at understanding what it is I am trying to say there will be other people around willing to translate.

This has become increasingly natural as the years go by and my audience is older and wiser. They are better able to gauge when and how they require assistance in understanding me. Also, as time goes by, I feel I have grown into my voice and am able to make myself understood better than I used to. (Even though when I hear myself back after recording various interviews I have absolutely no idea what it is I’m talking about!). This inbuilt technique has been effective when I am in concentrated social situations, such as in a pub and having a conversation with someone I do not know very well. I can mostly adopt verbal techniques which forces them to understand what it is I wish to say to them. Yet as good as this technique seems, it still remains very difficult to instigate conversation and establish a bond with someone who is foreign to the social group I find myself in.

Having said that, when I get drunk it becomes almost impossible to decipher anything I'm saying. It is total gibberish!

Starting middle school was the first time this social issue of communicating had been highlighted to me and the people who supported me. So I was delighted to discover that my form class teacher was someone who had been known to me since I was young. It was agreed that prior to the start of middle school, my new teacher, Graham Thorne would visit me at my home in order to familiarise himself with me and my requirements. Graham arguably had an advantage over his colleagues through knowing me all my life, as a result of us being within the same community and him mixing in the same social circle as my Mum and Dad.

This meant that on my arrival at middle school, all the teachers knew exactly how to treat me as they had been briefed by Graham and could assist my integration with other pupils. It wasn't long before I developed yet another friendship circle with likeminded friends who were also able to look beyond my disability and become advocates of my social inclusion, thus setting an example to the wider school community that it was acceptable to befriend someone like me. This attitude seemed to be contagious and soon everyone in the class wanted to be my friend. Was it for my handsome good looks? Boyish charm? Or was it merely the fact that I was different?

This newfound popularity came at a price as I did not want to get labelled as a mascot who everyone thought it was cool to say they were friends with. I hated people who came up to me and either uttered the words, "You've got a cool wheelchair Josh!" (I always thought wheelchairs were fashion neutral? Maybe I'm wrong!) Or even worse, thought we had something in common because one of their relatives was in a wheelchair. I couldn't care less about hearing stories of what they decorated their auntie's wheelchair with, why would I? They didn't want to hear about my

Gramps and his unsociable habits did they? Or maybe they did!

Therefore, for the first time in my relatively short life I was forced to be selective about who I befriended. This was not through arrogance, more survival and for the preservation of my self-respect. However, like I said, it wasn't long before I discovered new friends who I liked to think accepted me on the value of my personality and not just the extra bits which came with being my friend. Also they would in turn befriend Andy and as a result of our strong friendship, he and I had become almost inseparable.

If you ever saw me and Andy (or Ate my Father, as he's better known… he didn't actually eat my father but by the looks of him he could), out together you would realise it's less of a friendship, more of a marriage as we regularly argue like an old married couple. The basis of our relationship is each of us thinks the other is a bit of a twat but we've been friends for so long, we like that in each other. Also our tastes in entertainment is pretty much the same, although he insists he doesn't like Cilla Black, but I believe that's just to make him look cool!

Ever since I can remember, Andy and I have been equipped with a very specific sense of humour which not many people understand or appreciate. Even at the age of nine, it was very mature for our age. This made it very difficult when integrating ourselves into the social group as we were very aware that the rest of the members did not understand. While the rest of the group would be ranting and raving over WWF and films such as Cool Runnings, we would be more interested in Parkinson and Father Ted. I don't know how we found a middle ground with everyone else. Is there a correlation between Father Ted and Cool Runnings?

Apart from this slight difference in interests, my friendship circle were all very similar with the same dreams and aspirations of one day being successful in our chosen fields. As we grew a little older, everyone was thriving on their new found independence and were organising to meet up outside the school gate. This is when it hit home how different I was in relation to everyone else. Although mainstream school had allowed me to do everything without any boundaries, I believe this ability to 'travel' was the only aspect that no one had thought about when laying the foundations of my independence. Not that it was anyone's fault. I guess it was just life. Whenever a meeting place was arranged it was always my quest to be allowed to go there independently of an adult. However, as a result of the safety precautions required, my parents remained adamant that I should have a chaperone alongside me at all times. This was a subject I was to battle my Mum and Dad over for almost a decade.

In hindsight, I am able to empathise greatly with my parents in this aspect as if I was a parent and had a son who was as vulnerable as myself at such a young age, I would insist on keeping them safe at all times… it sounds obvious. However, for me at that specific time in my life all I wanted was my independence and I realised my mates had already got it, but somehow I could not. Do you remember when the latest toy or fad had arrived in the shops and everyone else had it but you were the last person to get it? This is exactly how I felt and it had a deep effect on me for years to come. It is something I have never really found a way to deal with.

No matter what I've achieved in my life or all the praise I get about not letting my disability get to me, I still find this issue hard to deal with and it has never gone away. Despite it no longer being as central as it was at school (or in gaining freedom from my parents), I still see a substantial gap between myself and the people I associate with. It's like the part of the jigsaw which never really fits. It's only at these times when I absolutely detest being in a wheelchair. Even though I had the support of figures around me, I had never felt so alone and useless as I did when my friends at school wanted to meet up somewhere and I couldn't. (Sorry, tissues are not supplied with this book!).

Over the years I have learnt how to control this feeling and attempt not to let it get in the way of anything I want to achieve. It's just part of me. Some may argue that this is the consequence of living a totally mainstream life with mainstream expectations and mainstream outcomes and in a way I would agree. Maybe in this situation I would have been far more content if I had befriended a social group made up of people with similar conditions to myself? You might actually be shouting that at this page right now. However, life is not always about accepting what you've got. If you don't challenge the way that you're perceived and treated, how will you ever grow as a person? I found myself in a group of very active friends and realised that they would want to do things that I couldn't. I realised that I would have to cope with the downsides of a mainstream life and in this situation the downside was not being able to do everything that my friends were allowed to. An important life lesson.

It's funny, I never get down or depressed about not being able to walk unaided or the inability to feed myself. Likewise, it doesn't bother me that my speech is hard to understand to the untrained ear or that I can't even wipe my own arse. What really gets me down, the bit about my disability that I hate the most, is not having the social independence to be part of the gang. Just the ability to sink into the crowd. When I'm in a pub I often look around at the men who are of a similar age to me and watch the way they carry themselves. How they interact with people they don't know and how two guys can have that universal understanding of each other without knowing anything about one another's life. It's so easy for people to generate that spark that gives them a common ground, but for me I know that I have to work hard at interaction. In order to do this, I find it easier being the joker and making light of the situation in order to put people at ease. Just like those people I meet in my professional life who understand that I have a lot to offer, it's always very rewarding when I'm in a social situation and people just get the fact that I am able to contribute like anyone else. I love to hit it off with people who don't need prewarning about my mental capacity, someone who could just treat me like anyone else and we could enjoy a normal conversation about football, ugly women, or how shit the beer is in this pub.

I guess this sense of acceptance is something which I have spent my whole life waiting for and is still one aspect of my situation which bothers me. On the occasions when my disability does get me down, I often ponder if my attitude was always the best for every situation I encountered. Sometimes I would really love just to forget about the limitations which my disability puts on me and engage in some sort of freedom. Life is not always safe, but people take that chance everyday irrespective of their physical requirements.

It was a hard situation, as on the outside it looked like myself and my parents wanted totally different things; I desperately wanted to be allowed to go out with my friends independently. My parents wanted me to have fun and enjoy similar experiences to my peers in a safe and consistent environment. Whereas on the inside, in retrospect, all parties just wanted me to be happy and content with what I had.

Towards the end of middle school, at the age of thirteen, this situation became even worse. As most of my circle of friends were very athletic, they would always meet at the park where they would play football, rugby or the obligatory schoolboy game of 'it'. So, whatever they did, involved some sort of physical activity, something which I would struggle doing even at the best of times, let alone without the assistance of an adult or carer. Speaking to Steve (my carer you first met in Chapter 2) about these times, he always says that this was the most difficult, as I thought my friends were more capable than they actually were. I think it was because I was much smaller than the rest of the group and I assumed that they naturally could move me, not taking into account their lack of strength. I thought whatever Steve could do, they could too. So Steve was always forced to be present in order to ensure I remained safe. But it wasn't Steve's relationship and the only time that I could be alone with my mates was in my bedroom full of wheelchairs, standing frames and posters of Cilla Black! Why would they want to be there?

When I look back at that time in my life, it is always with a certain amount of sadness and frustration that I couldn't be what I wanted to be. I couldn't fit in with the crowd. Not that I always wanted to follow the crowd. In fashion, interests or trends I've always prided myself on being slightly original, even separate from the pack as a result of my unique interests. Not everyone would dress up as Cilla Black, would they? Yet sometimes, it would have been rewarding to obtain a handful of the experiences which were open to my mates during this time. I felt totally unrelated from the world that they lived in and felt left out when hearing about spur of the moment activities that they all shared. I think this had a greater impact on me than I had thought and highlighted the huge difference between me and everyone else at that moment.

As we reached the verges of adulthood (around seventeen) the situation became far easier for me, as not only did I have time to reflect and reason about my own limitations, but my friends were also more responsible and capable of involving me in whatever they were doing. If there was a game of football arranged, one of them would always run me around after the ball in order for me to feel a part of it. Ironically, in later years one of my best friends from this era became my fulltime carer for the best part of three years. As a result of growing up with me he knew my needs and was able to fulfil the role in a perfect manner. But writing this now I can see that the feeling of being a little bit different from the crowd has never really gone away. Yes, it got a lot better when we were older, but the feelings of not quite being the same as everyone else, not having that universal ability and sharing in that union of physical freedom, has remained as a demon in my own head. I don't think it will ever, truly be able to get out.

During this period of frustration, I often recall people telling me to wait a couple of years. Wait until my friendship circle was a little older in order to be responsible. Wait until we could enjoy the social freedom which would come to surround us. But why? Why did I have to wait? Bloody hell, my life is all about waiting; waiting to go to the toilet, waiting for a carer to come round, waiting for the latest piece of equipment, why did I have to wait to socialise? At the time it was impossible to think of a future when I would be able to enjoy a mainstream social life. Yet the strange thing was, when it did happen and my friends were old enough and responsible enough to invite me out, there was no big fanfare. It just happened. Therefore, it is very difficult to pinpoint an exact time when my social independence began but when it did, it felt so good.

Although that 'moment' is difficult to pinpoint, I do know that the beginning of my A-levels saw big changes for me in terms of my social identity, mainly due to the fact that the sixth form at my high school had a common room. This meant all sixth form pupils could congregate there, both at break time and free periods. The tight confines of the room meant that students mixed together in very close proximity and therefore were forced to get to know a wider group of people. This benefitted me greatly as I could get to know people in an intimate environment without having to follow a crowd. For the first time since the era of 'The Den' I felt accepted in a mainstream social group and realised I had to take this opportunity to forge new friendships.

It wasn't just at school that I was finding new friends. In a bid to earn money during the university holidays, my sister, Lauren worked as a waitress in a local pub with the added bonus of her then boyfriend being the deputy manager. It didn't take me long to experience the pub for myself and discover that the friendly atmosphere was something that greatly appealed to me. Before long I was on speaking terms with the whole staff. I found I could relate to these people and realised that we had a lot in common, including a very warped sense of humour. So, when they invited me to join the pub pool team (don't worry, I never held a pool cue, before you wonder how many people I injured) I was so excited to be a part of this 'new gang'.

Naturally, given the location of the pool team, it was now that I properly discovered alcohol, although I had been teasing myself with it from the age of thirteen. At first it was difficult to find a beverage that didn't make me resemble a baby sucking on a lemon. My first tipple was a lager-top, (a lager topped off with lemonade) but if the lager was a little fizzy it would not only have a bad effect on my face but on my bladder too! I often recall getting home in the early hours of the morning doubled up in pain as a result of my desperation for the toilet. Yet this was inconsequential as finally, at last, I had done it, I had gone out with people of my own age, independent of an adult or carer and if that meant nearly pissing myself then it was totally worth it!

On reflection, this was possibly the greatest social era of my life, as all of my friends had (kind of) grown up and were entrusted by my parents to take me out on the town. However, on one occasion, near the end of my school life, I recall being at the main nightclub on the Island. All of a sudden, I was accosted by two men who put their feet under both sets of wheels of my wheelchair preventing me from wheeling myself away. I was on my way to the dance floor to follow some friends when this incident occurred, I could not move, felt totally helpless and did not know how I would attract anyone's attention. For about ten minutes these men were holding my wheels tightly and I was becoming increasingly panicked and irritated. In a desperate attempt to shake them off, I decided to punch them very hard in the bollocks which gave me enough time to scoot myself over to the others and replay the events. I was shitting myself.

This experience not only shook me up but reminded me of my vulnerability when in public places. I realised that I had been extremely lucky not to have been harmed that night. If these men had intended to hurt or kidnap me I would not have been in a position to put up a fight. (If only I was the spastic Jackie Chan!) I was consequently told that this could've been avoided if I'd had the presence of a carer to keep me safe. Yet I don't see this as the problem. It wasn't because I didn't have a carer present, it was more about my friends knowing that I am vulnerable; whilst I might love being one of the lads, I am different and someone has to look out for me. Unfortunately, I'd almost had to learn this lesson the hard way, but ever since that situation my friends and I have been increasingly aware of my vulnerabilities. Thankfully it has never happened again.

Now I'm not one of those "big girl's blouses" who won't confront their fears or allow an incident like that to make me become a recluse. Life is too short to be frightened of stuff. However, since that experience, I have always preferred a night out in a pub where I can be easily spotted and the noise levels are such that I can always be heard. Living on a small island has its benefits as most people from my home town either know me or know of me, meaning that wherever I go someone will be aware of my requirements. On the rare occasion that I do enter a nightclub, I always ensure that there is a responsible person pushing my chair so I don't feel so vulnerable. However, I still continue to go out without a carer in situations when I am in the company of old friends who know me really well and do not need the assistance of a third party. This is something I look forward to as for those few hours with my close friends, I feel like anyone else, independent of assistance or supervision. Just one of the lads.

Someone once described me as a social animal; there's nothing I like better than being in a room full of people chatting, laughing and bantering. I just love the feeling of bouncing off people and making them laugh. For some reason it's easier for me to do this when I don't have someone over my shoulder making sure that nobody trips over my wheelchair. Yet I don't care, if someone falls over me I just laugh and then get them to put me upright again. That's the risk I take to have this wonderful sense of freedom and it's definitely worth it!

This social freedom I thought would continue through and beyond university. Yet when I arrived in Bournemouth I realised that the geographical area would of course not be conducive to this kind of social situation. Situated out of town, it wasn't easy for the students from our course to socialise and people tended to make friends with others in their halls. This was difficult for me as I lived in disabled accommodation with mature students living upstairs. It wasn't anyone's fault but I was isolated away from all the action and there was very little I could do about it. If I didn't have my next-door neighbour to keep me company I would have been so lonely. This triggered a lot of thoughts which remain as squatters inside my mind: maybe I cannot fit into the mainstream after all, maybe I just got lucky with the friends I made in school, maybe they just pitied me.

University is a very strange place to be. For the first few weeks no one really knows anyone, everyone is trying to suss everyone else out and select who appeals to them, a bit like animals in a cage. So, having a severe disability together with communication difficulties, I was always going to be the feral animal sitting watching, whilst the rest of them went about trying to make sense of their environment. It felt as if nobody knew how to interact with me and many were scared to even try. Subsequently, it stopped me from making an effort with them because I knew how uncomfortable they were feeling. Also, there was only so much I knew about Star Trek and Battlestar Galactica, so I figured I would not have much of an input. Therefore, my three years on my undergraduate course were very lonely, I say this with no disrespect to Steve & Gray who were there for me, it just wasn't what I'd hoped Uni would be in terms of creating a new social circle of friends. Although I was just happy being a comedy geek.

When I decided to embark on a Master's degree and return to Bournemouth University for what would be a fourth year on campus, I was already resigned to the fact that my social life would be, again, non-existent. Bloody hell, if I couldn't get a conversation out of anyone in three years, I doubted anything would change in just 12 months! To my surprise, because of the diverse range of people on the course, including in age, race, religion and gender, it meant there was an unspoken universal acceptance of everyone. This echoed throughout the whole framework of directors, producers and editors. It seemed everyone was a little more grown-up (I say grown-up, there definitely wasn't a grown-up approach to our social life) and ready to integrate themselves in order to make the most of the whole experience. At last, I was where I belonged.

During the second term, it was revealed that we would be taking part in a cross-platform program which offered students the opportunity to collaborate with people from other courses within the framework. This gave me the ideal opportunity to get to know members of the group very well and likewise offered them time to realise that we had a lot in common. We all shared the same bizarre X-rated sense of humour and our laughter was very contagious. It could be said that this group definitely promoted multiculturalism and diversity as there were members from all over the world, as far flung as Thailand, South Africa, France, Ireland and good old England. You would think this would have been a huge barrier for me and my disability to overcome, as a result of such diverse cultures, yet it was actually a match made in heaven.

Myself and a South African called Graeme, represented the writing talent and it wasn't until we were put together within this group that we realised how much we had in common. Up until then, he and I had merely enjoyed a polite acquaintance and he later confessed to not knowing how to interact with me or whether in fact his interaction would have been well received. It was a shame that we had wasted so much time in being polite when we could have enjoyed a much longer friendship. If only we had understood each other's preconceptions. Yet when we began to get to know each other, it didn't take us long to realise how similar we were, including our mutual love for alcohol and making fun of people, which would occupy hours and hours of our time. Actually, our friendship was built on the ability to take the piss out of everyone else which we found so appealing. It was clear that I had found a kindred spirit.

I always love it when I can make a connection with someone without the need for a third-party involvement. As soon as I met Graeme I realised we had a spark. We both laughed at the same infantile nonsense and shared a love of the random, childish things in life. So when I saw him, in the lecture theatre, rolling up balls of blue tack to mischievously throw at unsuspecting members of our group, I realised that we were going to get along. That was the start of a magical friendship which I hope will now last forever. Establishing this friendship meant so much to me. For the first time I hadn't had anyone else do the leg work for me. I'd made a great friend on my own merit and it felt amazing.

At last I had a person who could be the advocate for my social interactions and when Graeme was familiar to the way I interacted with people, he was able to pass it on to the rest of the group. Before long, they realised that they too could interact with me in the same way as Graeme did. This was helped by the other English member of the group who came from the Midlands and had an additional advantage by understanding my speech. This proved a very useful tool in bridging the gap between me and the rest of the group as there were now two people who were comfortable with translating to the others. However, it wasn't long before the whole group became accustomed to understanding my utterances which was a breakthrough for my social life at university.

It was amazing to think these people, from all over the world who for some, English was their second language, could understand and even translate my speech with ease. Some of the people I have known all my life who are native to my mother-tongue were not even up to this level of interaction. It was almost unbelievable that figures from around the world could enjoy this intensive level of social interaction with me, to the extent we produced academic work to a very high standard. It was obvious that although very different in our appearance, the whole team adhered to an unspoken common ethic.

Finally these were people on my wavelength. I thought I would have spent another year just with Steve and Gray for company (which wasn't a problem but I am sure that even we would eventually run out of bullshit to talk about!) However, it was a nice surprise to find people who understood and echoed my personality. Also, in terms of productivity it really benefits you when you're in a group of like-minded people because you bounce off each other and are never without inspiration. The second term of my Masters was probably the best of my Uni experience as I just felt a part of something, not just in my work but as a whole social network. We were able to create and produce a cross-platform children's resource which could be used as either a TV programme, a website or a podcast. It was even viewed by the BBC. This proved that a fully functioning team which all got on, could actually create something to industry standards. Yet beyond this we had become very good friends which I believe was the most important thing to come from it.

Our strong friendship did not end at the lecture theatre and we were able to develop quite a rich social life. This was a new experience for me, as finally I was able to taste the other side of being a student and realised that with this extra aspect to my university life I felt complete and enriched. I attended house parties, midweek football matches at the pub, organised takeaway nights at my student flat and even 90's nights at the Student Union. Particularly with Graeme, we never missed a televised midweek football game which obviously included several rum and cokes. This feeling spurred me onto a happy and enjoyable climax to the whole university experience. Finally I could say that I had lived a typical student life, thanks to both the friends that I had made during my Masters and the laid back attitude of my care team, who were the perfect complement to my social and academic activities.

At the close of my university experience, our diverse and intimate social group was to disperse as we all returned to our respective homes throughout the world. It was a very unique time in a very unique place which sadly may never happen again. However, modern technology means that wherever you are in the world you are only a Skype call away from a friend. This group will occupy a special place in my heart as all of them in their own way were able to teach me that it is possible to create a strong bond with people who do not necessarily know your background. Also, I did this all on my own, without the requirement of known figures in order to make it acceptable for them to befriend me. It was solely my relationship and one that I feel most proud of.

On my return to the Isle of Wight, I thought that my social life would continue to flourish with the added complement of having familiar people around me. However, I was shocked to find that this was not the case and in fact I was in a worse situation than I had been at university. By this time, all the members of my friendship circle had flown the nest and were living in various areas around Britain. So, from a personal perspective, I felt somewhat alone without the network of support to which I had grown increasingly accustomed. However, in recent years, since being fully reinstated on the Island, I have managed to find great friends who are local and regularly meet up with them. As I get older I have met friends in the most random places and it's great to have such different pockets of people so my social calendar is frequently full. For someone who was once so paranoid about being able to be part of the gang I am now a member of several!

At the end of the day, I just love being sociable, that's my drug! In any social arena, you will always find me right at the centre of hilarity and fun. I like to think I am the life and soul of the party and the way I have adapted how I see myself has helped me to become just that. I think my disability should never be a barrier to me doing the things I want to do and it definitely will never effect my ability to have a good time.

VIII

Window Shopping

Before we start this next chapter, for those of you who think you've just picked up Gok Wan's autobiography by mistake… you haven't. This is the bit where I shall get rather analytical about myself and the way others see me. Wherever I go or whatever I do, I sense people make assumptions without even knowing anything about me. Therefore, when I meet people I find myself working twice as hard to make sure that they know there is a light on upstairs!

The idea for this book came to me when I was visiting my sister when she lived in Worcester. I clearly remember being in a shopping outlet and everyone who walked past stared at me. Instead of getting embarrassed or irritated I began to think about what must have been going through their heads? What did they think of me? I would have loved to know what they thought my life would be like. Not because I cared about what they thought of me, but because I was fascinated to find out how they thought my life would be, from just seeing me in the street.

It then occurred to me that whenever I step foot outside of my own home, I am the subject of fascination. No, it's not my uncanny resemblance to Jude Law or David Beckham as I often think. It's actually because I'm probably sat in my wheelchair, moving, dribbling and speaking, or what many believe, just making noises. It's a difficult concept to get over to strangers that despite the dribbling and the moving, I am actually all there… well, some people would argue with that. Strangers passing by just see a little snapshot of my life and create an image of the severity of my disability.

It is very difficult to establish what it is that they find so fascinating, even to this day when diversity and disability are both hot topics on political agendas. Since the rise of political correctness during the early 1980s, the subjects of disability and diversity seem to have become taboo in the media and in general conversation. Typically British, we don't like to talk about anything that might be a little controversial and so there seems to be an unexplained void in communicating how disabled people want to be treated. Therefore, when I go to a restaurant it is the norm that the waiter will ask whoever is sat next to me what I would like to eat. Hello! I have a menu in front of me and I can read! Surely you can ask me what I want for my dinner?

Despite Britain as a whole becoming more accepting in their attitude towards disability, it is only when one encounters a stranger and witnesses their bizarre behaviour towards someone like me, that I realise there is still a great deal of misconception and prejudice regarding disability. Whenever I am in the centre of my local town's shopping area, I can always be sure that there will be a person who thinks they are doing a good deed in coming over to me and either holding my hand or patting me on the head, or even greeting me with a patronising statement. Firstly, I am not a dog and why is it socially acceptable to pat a spastic on the head? If someone did that to an able-bodied person, the 'Patter' would probably spend the next three months in intensive care, so why is it socially acceptable to do that to me? It gets worse; some even end their well-meaning crusade by turning to whoever is accompanying me and saying, "You're doing a great job." How do they know? Are they a psychic? For all they know, my 'companion' could then take me into a dark alley and kick the hell out of me, but nevertheless, to the stranger they are doing a great job. (Except they wouldn't because I'm triple hard - I'm like the disabled Tom Hardy!)

My Mum often recalls an occasion when, at the age of twelve, I was involved in selling raffle tickets on the high street with my local Sea Scout troop, when an elderly lady came over and offered to buy me an ice cream. My Mum replied, "Yes, they would all like one." So this unfortunate elderly lady was forced to buy ice cream for the whole troop. That is what you call equal opportunities! When reading this you would be excused for thinking ill of my mother for taking advantage of an old woman in this way, to spend her hard-earned pension on five ice creams for children. Yet for my Mum and everyone involved with me, it was more than that. This was to prove a point. I was no different from any other child in that situation and therefore, if the elderly woman wanted to buy me an ice cream, she should have wanted to buy everyone an ice cream. It was obvious that this specific woman lacked the ability to perceive me as a normal child. Having said that, is it ever normal for young children to dress up as sailors and attend a two-hour club every week?

I was just trying to be 'normal' and I was definitely not a token member of the group. I was not simply there to make up the numbers or boost the inclusive attitude of the Sea Scouts. Although in reality, this may have been the perception of many people. I was very conscious of the fact that I did not want to appear as a token member of anything. I wanted to be a needed and valued member of the group. Well, no, not even that, I just wanted to have fun with my friends.

From an early age it was instilled in me that there would be no room for special treatment or allowances. I understood that in order to live in a mainstream world I was expected to adhere to mainstream rules and values. This forced me to develop devices and techniques which would put me on a par with my peers and I was treated with the same amount of care and respect as them. This was very difficult to explain to both parents and children if they had not had the exposure to someone like me before. So, in this respect once the children realised that I could be treated in exactly the same manner as them, they were ironically leading their parents about how to interact with someone like me and were very comfortable in doing so.

The school environment was probably the first arena where I was consciously aware of the fact that people were staring at me. For an adult this would have been somewhat disconcerting, making them feel extremely uncomfortable. But for me, I guess I just got used to it. So, when there was a new child at the school, I knew that for the first couple of days I would be the subject of great fascination until they got it out of their system and the novelty wore off. The only situation which did irritate me was when those children who knew me carried on following me around just staring at me, like I was an animal in a cage or an alien that had just stepped off a spaceship. Surely they had better things to do with their lunch break rather than just following me around?

Indeed, it wasn't only the children who felt they should in some way interact with me. As the only pupil in the whole school with an obvious disability, I was known to the whole staff. Whenever I was spotted in the corridors, I would always become inundated with people saying hello, which in time, led to the head teacher advising the staff they need not go out of their way to talk to me. After all, they didn't do it to anyone else. I began to feel that I was blending into the crowd and although it was still obvious to all that I was different from the other children, it created the illusion that it was possible for me to become anonymous. Of course I wasn't anonymous at all. Sat in an electric metal wheelchair with a massive tray which held an array of brightly coloured light switches - even Stevie Wonder would have been aware of me!

There was an obvious difference in the manner in which the adults would interact with me as opposed to the relaxed and natural attitude of the other children. When situations arose with children who were unfamiliar to me, they often became uncomfortable with the situation and relied on an adult to communicate with me. Unbeknown to me, this technique would be one I would have to rely on throughout my life. This remains one of my most successful communicative devices to date and became vital for those children who adopted an extra unusual interest in me. They'd usually follow me around the school until either Soph or one of my friends would get rid of them for me. I wasn't a model in an exhibition nor a public statue. I was more than happy for people to come over and say hello if they actually wanted to be my friend but I wasn't going to be the school's national heritage site!

As I grew into adulthood I realised this unwanted fascination with my disability didn't end at the school gates. Irrespective of where I went, I could sense people staring and looking at me. As a fresh-faced youth who did not hold the desire to categorise himself in any way, certainly not by his disability, this became very disconcerting and forced me to question my identity. I clearly remember thinking that it was strange but I didn't yet have the ability to conceptualise it. Yet going into adulthood, this feeling of being different has never gone away and now lays dormant inside my mind only to be rediscovered in moments of frustration and crisis.

Prior to encountering a social minority, people can have very strict preconceptions about diversity and disability. I often recall a specific occasion when Soph came to visit me at university and arranged to meet up with a friend she had known whilst in Brighton. Having never met me before and merely hearing Soph's description of me, in which she purposefully omitted the fact that I had a disability, the girl imagined that I was just the average Joe. We arranged to meet her in the Student Union which was ideally situated on campus, one minute away from my student house. Soph met her at the door of the bar and guided her over to our table where she was very shocked to find that I was indeed disabled. Instantly, a sense of shock and embarrassment came over her face and she was unable to participate in any social interaction and eventually made her excuses and left. This remains the strangest reaction I have ever witnessed.

Her reaction may seem a little bit extreme to some of you, following the issues which have already been discussed in this book. However if one was to adopt an empathic approach towards the woman, who was led to believe that I was just a normal twenty-three year old guy who was on a night out, you could excuse it for shock. Why would it even enter her head that this person may be disabled? It was just a shame she didn't stick around long enough to have her preconceptions and prejudices challenged and maybe even reversed. Of course I am looking at it from a biased point of view, as that is all I've ever known. I've been lucky that most people have been able to put their preconceptions to one side and see me for who I am. But if someone is unable to do that, they shouldn't be chastised for it. Maybe she couldn't handle my sexual magnetism?

Changing the perception of me has become increasingly easier and more comfortable over the years. It seems that almost every stranger who comes into contact with me needs to learn that other than my obvious physical differences, I exhibit equal amounts of emotional and mental capacity as the normal man. It sounds a bit pretentious and phony but I think it's a vital lesson for anyone who really wants to get to know me. More recently, when I returned from university, we were forced to interview for a full-time carer. The successful candidate did not even have eye-contact with me throughout the whole interview. However, despite this I realised that there was something about him that appealed to me, so I decided to take a punt. Soon after he started working with me, he was able to realise that I was his intellectual equal and has now become one of my most successful personal assistants.

The carer in question, James, has since explained that if he had known more about my condition and my mental capacity, then he would have been more inclined to interact with me sooner. I think that is one of the major things that is overlooked when people are introducing me to others. Because they are already so comfortable in the way I communicate, they sometimes forget that it's difficult for someone that doesn't know me. Maybe if more 'veterans' of the art of understanding me shared their techniques with people who were less confident, or indeed totally naive to me and my situation, then maybe more people would feel comfortable in having a conversation with me.

This is further evidence to suggest that onlookers should not take a disabled person on face value. It can prove very frustrating for me when I see those curious people in the street, who stare at me or speak to me as if I'm an infant. They don't know me, they don't know that I have a Master's Degree and I am mentally sound. All they see is a shell of a person who exhibits no individuality or personality, just a generic disabled person who people should feel sorry for and pour pity on like syrup on a pancake. There could be a number of reasons why people find it necessary to have this reaction towards me; maybe they've had emotional trauma surrounding a disabled person, maybe it's because of some sort of regret surrounding disability in the past or maybe they've actually been disabled themselves.

Alternatively, if one should adopt James' first impression, one finds it increasingly easier to reverse expectations and highlight the fact that I am in fact part of mainstream society. If they can do this and leave their preconceptions where they found them, then they realise that in every way I am just an average human being. Yet people who meet me on a fleeting basis or have a snapshot of me being wheeled down the high street with dribble on my face are less likely to overcome their prejudices. This does not affect me at the time but I often feel empathy for them, in that if they encounter a disabled person they lack the initiative to overcome such a social hurdle.

Sometimes I do wonder just how many people will believe that I'm the writer of this book. When you picked it up, with the cover closed, how would you have reacted if somebody had told you that a dribbly, spasming man in a wheelchair has spent hours upon hours tapping away with his nose on an iPad? Would you have believed it? Would anybody actually believe that I wrote this book or would they think I was merely present while a nurse wrote it on my behalf, in between topping up my drip? These are just some of the things that I would love to know… What really goes through people's minds when thinking about people in my situation?

People can be forgiven for harbouring these preconceptions as a result of limited exposure to and insight into people such as myself. It can prove very hard to differentiate between a person with a physical handicap, to those who exhibit mental challenges and even I have to admit to having similar preconceptions when I see other disabled people in the street. There is a fine line between treating everyone as equals and going beyond someone's mental or physical capacity, which could result in embarrassment for both the good willed stranger and the disabled person. I would prefer to have a universal understanding where, if you are not known to such a person, you treat them as any other stranger and in the words of the legendary Dionne Warwick, "Walk on by…"

Luckily, this misconception of 'tokenism' is not shared by all and most of the time strangers are more than tolerant to my situation. They understand that if key people are able to interact with me wholeheartedly, it must not be that hard to pick up. It proves far easier to overcome this social hurdle when my interaction with a stranger is in a quiet setting where it is easier to understand me. People have always stated that their biggest worry is the fear of not understanding what I am saying and the uncomfortable situation it may create for both parties. Yet, as I have stated previously, repeating myself is something that never bothers me and providing that the listener is doing just that, I do not mind how many times I am asked to repeat myself (as apparent in this book!) In overcoming this common misconception, I find myself becoming increasingly vivacious when faced with a group of new people, providing I have a key person to translate. This technique breaks down the barriers and is a signal to the untrained ear that I am not precious about my disability. In fact, I regularly attempt to make a mockery of it to reinforce that reality. This either makes the listener realise that they are interacting with someone who is intellectually and emotionally their equal, or makes them feel even more uncomfortable about me. Moreover, this technique actually gave me the inspiration for the title of this book, as throughout my life I think I have adapted both my physical capabilities and my language techniques in order to simplify and make accessible interactions between myself and others.

Hopefully, by reading this book people will identify with my struggles with communication and misrepresentation. Maybe you know of someone who is disabled and you have always steered away from instigating interaction with them for fear of being stumped if there was to be a communication breakdown. Yet if you were able to forget about your preconceptions and start up a conversation, you may be shocked to find a like-minded person somewhere among the wheels and dribble. However, please don’t go out of your way to talk to them just because you feel you should. Just understand that more than likely they will just want to get on with their business as discreetly as you do and whatever you do, don't pat them on the head or offer to buy them an ice cream!

IX

The Three Degrees

A book about the biggest achievements in life would not be complete without a chance to dissect my university experience. After all, not a day goes by without someone stopping me in the street with the phrase, "What a massive achievement that you went to university!" Or, "Are you still at college?" (I know I'm not the brightest but ten years doing a degree is a bit long... even for me! And being as we're getting technical, it wasn't college, it was a university!). From a young age I always had the passion to go to university. I was determined to cultivate a craft and be accepted for that rather than lowering my expectations of myself just because I had Cerebral Palsy. As you must have gathered by now, to me my disability played no part in determining the life that I would have and I was certain that I was never going to let that change.

Since the age of thirteen, there was only ever one university for me: Bournemouth had the only degree course solely on the art of scriptwriting. I remember trawling through the old UCAS books trying to find other places that offered something similar to Bournemouth but I never found anything. Scriptwriting was the only thing I wanted to do and Bournemouth was the only place to go. Even after my first fact-finding visit to campus it felt like it was the bedrock of media and I instantly knew I'd found my place!

I can clearly remember A-Level results day. Di turned up at my house ridiculously early ready to push me to school. That walk was one of the longest walks of my whole life and it was only round the corner! Arriving at school it was a scramble to find my envelope and then we had a further wait while we negotiated our way through the massive queue which had developed behind us. Getting outside, Di opened the envelope and turned the paper round for me to read it first. I got a B and a C - enough to get into Bournemouth! I was so thrilled, I just wanted to shout it from the rooftops. All that work and dedication had paid off and I was going to Bournemouth - I couldn't wait!

My four years at university resulted in me obtaining both a Bachelor of Arts in Scriptwriting for Film and Television and a Masters in Writing for the Media. If you're like me, you've probably completely switched off after that last sentence. After all, what does it mean? It just means I spent four years pratting about and not getting on with my life. Yet I believe I learnt a lot about how to live independently (well sort of!). Living on my own was something that appealed greatly to me. I was looking forward to not having to play by someone else's rules all the time. I just thought it would be a combination of working hard all day and partying hard at night. However, I still can't work out how accurate that perception actually was.

So as this is a book about my greatest achievements and my positive attitude towards my disability, I feel that my university experience gave me an insight into what the rest of my life would look like in terms of my care requirements and gave me the ability to manage them. This was a big eye opener for me as I had previously relied upon Mum and Dad to have those uncomfortable conversations. They always led the care management procedures but being so many miles away from home, we realised that this wouldn't be possible. So it was agreed that we would hire an agency to manage my care package.

For the very first time I was in touch with a social worker who created a care plan for me with questions such as, 'How many times a day do you visit the toilet?' My answer was, 'Depends what I have eaten the night before.' Why does someone like me even need a care plan? I was at university. I knew how to look after myself, I just needed someone to do the things I couldn't. If I needed a prescribed care plan then maybe I shouldn't have been there in the first place? It was utterly ludicrous!

On reflection, the decision to hire an agency to manage all care issues was a knee-jerk reaction to a brand-new situation. Mum and Dad figured that if they couldn't be in the vicinity to keep an eye on my care, then an agency seemed like the perfect option. If we had truly known the extent of the limitations that an agency would put on my life, we would have never pursued that avenue. However, the university seemed to have a very strong relationship with the specific agency and this impression reassured myself and my parents that all services were one big happy family, so what could go wrong? In hindsight the answer to that question is too long to describe within the parameters of this book.

The summer before university, the care agency made a complimentary trip down to the Isle of Wight for a meeting regarding the setup of my care over the next twelve months. They also brought down two potential applicants for the job as my carer, who were interviewed by me and my parents. At first glance they looked more like builders than carers and if they hadn't been with the manager of the agency I would have thought they were local handymen. Both of these guys were a lot older than me, closer to Mum and Dad's generation than mine. How are you meant to get a flavour of someone in half an hour?

Making up the third member of this care team was a familiar face; the former barman at my local pub. On reflection, this has to be up there with the most bizarre carer appointments I have ever made. During my farewell party at a country pub in a sleepy village on the coast of the Isle of Wight, I had invited an old acquaintance from my brief time as a mascot for the pool team. As a teenager I looked up to Rick as a key person who understood how to facilitate my social life. We had met a couple of years previously when Lauren got some casual work as a waitress in the pub where he worked. In the space of a few years, we had enjoyed many things together; camping, lock-ins at pubs and even crazy golf. We knew each other well and I regarded Rick among my closest friends. When he arrived at the party, I started to inform him of the dubious efforts of the care agency, he automatically offered his services to which I wholeheartedly agreed. It was a bizarre agreement but exactly what I needed!

Having never ever thought about a career in care, this was a brand-new situation for Rick and even though we had got to know each other really well over the past three years, he had never really had to help me with any personal care. However he had seen me doing what I do best; socialising with a big group of friends in a pub. He realised what I wanted out of life and together I knew that we would have a lot of fun. This was vital to my perseverance during my first year of uni and Rick remained a constant throughout. It felt reassuring to have a figure whom I shared history to comfort me in times of stress and provide me with support through the unpredictable situations which I faced. Also, knowing that there was a figure within my care team who for all intents and purposes was a family friend, made the care agency cautious as to their actions when he was present.

Having Rick's support meant that I could actually go ahead and do what I was there to do. Indeed it wasn't only my care requirements which needed delicate management.

After the best part of fifteen years of Di and Penny carefully and lovingly organising my education, I slowly realised that I may no longer have such bespoke support and I just hoped that my new academic team shared the same ethic. I wanted to show people that I could work independently of known figures and still achieve my academic potential. I felt that there were still some people who assumed that Di and Penny did all my work for me and I was just a bystander. When we met the additional learning support team, it was obvious that they wanted to understand everything about my life so they could work out the best way to support me. Originally it was decided that a team of three would be the best system to work with me, in shifts of one or two. Having a high turnover of staff, it was discovered early on that this intimate team wouldn't be able to sustain all of my education requirements. Eventually I ended up working with a grand total of thirty-three educational support workers during my first year and for someone who had spent their whole school life with the same two people, this came as a great shock.

Still having yet to master how to write with my nose on an iPad, I relied upon my educational team to help me with almost every task attributed to my studies. Back then my preferred technique was to dictate to a scribe who would write it on a sheet of paper before handing it to a typist who would tap it into the computer. For some reason I preferred this system as it allowed me to instantly read what had been scribed and I could make relevant changes as soon as I spotted them. This system proved reliable until the creation of my first university script when I needed to adhere to the script format on the computer which deemed my old system redundant. I had to learn very quickly how to direct people on a PC which was not only great for my skill set but also did wonders for the learning support budget!

This support was funded by my local education authority and was heavily structured around my learning requirements. Therefore, I not only had a university timetable detailing lectures and seminars but I also had to notify the learning support department when I requested to work on my assignments. If only I had conquered the art of writing with my nose on an iPad, then I could have carried out my assignments whenever I wanted without the need for scheduled assistance. It's interesting to think how different my university life would have been if Apple had developed this great technological tool earlier. How would it have affected the help I received? How did anyone expect me to limit my creativity to six hours a day? Although hours in the evenings and weekends were offered, it was hard to know when I would have that spark of creativity which made me want to write stuff down. How does anyone know when they're gonna get a good idea? I'm just so thankful for my iPad now and knowing that I have the ability to write my thoughts down whenever I like without limitations.

I really enjoyed my time with my educational team. As great as the lectures and seminars were, I began to really look forward to carrying out my work solely with one person taking down my utterances. It was at these moments when I felt at my most creative. I could forget about my problems with a blank page, I was free to go anywhere my mind would take me. This reinforced the real purpose of university and I just wanted more.

Having this bespoke educational support encouraged me to think positively about university. Yet as a mere eighteen-year old I understandably lacked the social confidence to manage and direct two different teams of people. It felt like I had no let-up in telling people what I wanted and with no familiarity around me, I made the mistake of relying on both of these groups for emotional support. In hindsight I realise that this was a big mistake as instead of bringing about cohesion to my life, it just brought resentment and I felt it was all my fault. If I was going through the same experiences now, I would keep my cards very close to my chest. I've learned when to and when not to confide in people and the severe disadvantages of people knowing too much. But at eighteen-years old and just having left home, I'm sure I can be excused for having such social naivety.

It was a very difficult process to get my head around because I was required to interact with so many different people: my three carers, the care agency, a social worker, my educational team, the learning support department, course leaders and not forgetting my peers. I was used to meeting and socialising with a whole host of different people and never had a problem in getting my voice heard. Yet somehow this was different. It was like the life had been sucked out of me and I couldn't find my tongue. It felt like I didn't fit with university life and I knew that everyone was treading on egg shells around me. This wasn't me. I'd always been so gutsy and never let anything get the better of me. So why could I not tell people what was wrong? Was it some sort of depression? Or had I just realised that I wasn't cut out for university?

Whenever I get down or upset, the only thing which guarantees me mental freedom is my ability to write. It's my sanctuary! I know that while I'm being creative, everything else is blocked out and I don't think about anything other than the words which are going on the page. So what better way to forget about my troubles than to write? I was always comforted to know that for six hours per day I had the incredible opportunity to do what I loved. Even now when I get in my creative zone it's like the rest of the world disappears and I can forget my troubles and be whoever I want to be. This was a godsend at the time and I treated it like emotional therapy.

With my educational life flourishing, a series of unfortunate events created a vacancy within my care team which the agency had a responsibility to fill as soon as possible. Meanwhile, I was forced to have two young ladies share the hours between them until a replacement could be found. In any other circumstance, if an eighteen-year old boy is told that he is going to be showered by two young attractive blondes with big tits, he would be jumping for joy at the thought of all of his Christmases coming at once (literally)! However, this was not the way I saw it, as they were forced to carry out every task 'by the book' and as clinically as possible. Although it did mean I had an attractive companion on my arm for the Fresher's Ball (albeit the arm of my wheelchair).

This experience reinforced my reasoning for hiring male carers as in an emergency and without the assistance of a hoist, a female may have some reservations regarding their ability to lift me in a safe and consistent manner and I wouldn't feel comfortable with this situation either. To me it seemed a bit weird, relying on a woman for my physical requirements. I hope you don't think I'm taking a rule out of some blatantly sexist politician's book, but it just didn't feel right. It wasn't about a woman's ability to do the job, it was that I don't need further reminding of my physical limitations and I felt that a woman would automatically highlight this when it needn't be an issue. This is a subject that I will return to in a later chapter (the Sherlock's amongst you may have guessed which one when looking at the chapter headings).

Luckily for me, it wasn't long before another replacement had been found and I could once again think positively about my university experience. This is when I realised that in order for me to be productive, I'm required to be absolutely content with those around me. At school Penny and Di created an open and relaxed atmosphere where I felt like I could express myself however I wanted and knowing me so well they understood how to treat me in almost every situation. Naively I assumed that this would naturally happen with my team at university. Yet with separate identified roles, both my care and educational support teams lacked the cohesion to work alongside each other as a result of the clear boundaries set by each establishment. It felt cold and was something I'd never experienced before. I knew I didn't like it but by expressing a concern, I just made it worse. If only I realised that at the time then maybe I could have made it easier for myself, but being eighteen, it simply never occurred to me. I'm not sure I am adequately conveying the true turbulence of this time, but it was horrendous and on a daily basis I contemplated quitting Uni for good.

Yet help was on its way. Arriving at the end of the first term with no experience and being a few months younger than me, he seemed like a little bit of a risk. However, on meeting Nick, I realised that he was equipped with many qualities that I had enjoyed with my care team on the Isle of Wight. He was young, he was strong, and he was very determined to help me live exactly how I wanted and not what the agency had prescribed. Here was a figure that in some ways was able to resemble the same standard of care which I was familiar with. Finally there was someone new, who I could fully trust!

At last I was able to begin living the normal university life that Bournemouth had to offer. I could go out in the evening and maybe even taste some of the university alcohol which I had heard so much about from my friends at home. Nick even went against the agency's protocol and avoided using the hoist in order to make life more comfortable for me. Well it was a little bit of that, but mostly it was because he couldn't be bothered to move the hoist from the other end of the house to the toilet, so it actually made his life easier as well. We identified with each other's hopes and aspirations and this made it easier for us to create a strong bond. With Nick everything just felt right and I felt safe in his care and trusted him wholeheartedly to carry out any physical challenge with me.

This technique proved a successful formula for both him and me until we were asked to take part in a fire evacuation training day where both the agency and the learning support department were present. There were three disabled students with their respective entourages all gathered to learn the university's fire evacuation procedure. It looked more like a disabled version of "The Sopranos". But I was forced to keep my sarcastic comments to myself as this was a serious issue. When the fire steward asked for a volunteer to trial the evacuation chair I was the first to put my hand up and so became the guinea pig yet again! This became complicated when Nick got disciplined by the manager of the care agency for taking me out my chair with his bare hands and moving me on to the evacuation chair. What Nick didn't have the heart to tell her was that in the event of a real fire we would not even bother with the stupid chair, he would just chuck me over his shoulder and get out of the building as fast as his legs could carry us!

Luckily for me, Nick was able to remain as my full-time university carer for the best part of two years and both fulfilled and challenged my personal requirements. Suddenly I was able to think positively as a result of having such a capable and flexible figure at my side. Finally, I could involve myself in age appropriate activities such as selecting my FHM Top Ten Women of 2006 and drinking so much beer I almost wet myself, but of course I didn't because Nick could just about take me to the toilet anywhere. This was what university was all about and I intended to make the most of it.

Thankfully, when I returned home Rick and Calum agreed to share the summer hours between the two of them. This was exactly what I needed after such a turbulent year that had seen me close to abandoning university for good. This good news was further boosted by the fact that Nick had expressed an interest in returning to my care team at the start of the new academic year. Not that he had technically left my team, but with me being at home over the summer it was a much needed confidence boost to know that he would be by my side again when I returned to Bournemouth. I knew all of my requirements would be met to the very best of his ability.

During this time, the return of a long-term back injury meant Rick would be out of action for many months. Therefore, my parents and I surmised that as a result of his physical health it may not be viable for him to make a full recovery in order to facilitate my needs. We concluded that he would not want to risk doing more damage to his back when working with me. I felt this was a great loss to my Uni care team as Rick offered me stability and familiarity at a very turbulent time and without his vital involvement it is difficult to imagine that I would have completed my first year.

It was very hard to inform Rick that his services were no longer needed as he had not done anything wrong and in my eyes he always remained a very good carer. Besides this, we had enjoyed a very active friendship for a number of years and I am afraid to say this situation was to compromise our relationship for good. I hoped that in time he would realise that we made the decision based on his best interests and to protect his physical health. I often reflect upon this and conclude that not only did I lose a good carer but also a close friend. Even now, on the rare occasion when I encounter him in the street, we are unable to enjoy a comfortable and relaxed conversation as we both find ourselves a little on edge when it comes to interacting with one another. When you have this situation with someone who once knew you well, you feel a great sense of loss. You're both still going about your everyday life but that spark which once united you both is now dead and for me that is still very hard to accept.

In terms of regret, that is up there as one of the biggest of my life, not because I thought Rick would last forever, as in some situations a carer only has a limited shelf life and it becomes my responsibility to interpret when enough is enough. But, Rick was blessed with a perfect, selfless attitude which was able to cater for all my needs and promoted my independence as an adult. Something which I will never forget as I go on to work with a whole host of different carers. If he had been younger and fitter, I imagine he would have been the perfect carer and those qualities which he acquired would have made him invaluable to my care team for a very long time. But above all, he was a good friend.

I often reflect on this time and the manner in which Rick was forced to leave my team. He realised the importance of me being independent and believed that despite needing support I was free to live an independent life. He also never forced his opinions on what he thought I should do for the best. When I moved out of my mum and dad's home in 2012, I wondered how different it would have been if Rick had still been with me. Always challenging and reflecting upon the way I lived my life, he recognised that I had determination and along with his practical abilities I am sure we could have made the perfect partnership for many years. I hope that in time, we manage to meet up again and can enjoy a healthy friendship once more.

So, if my first year could be as dramatic as that, what did the second have in store? On the plus side I still had Nick who had been the only positive in my care team for the past eight months. It was agreed that my two home carers, Calum and Leo should accompany me down to Bournemouth in order to supply cover in the interim when I was without a full care team. Calum and Leo knew me so well and I felt completely safe with them. To have them by my side meant so much to me. Having Calum there was massive - of all the people in the world, he knew me the best and it made stepping back into my accommodation that little bit easier. It felt like a different place.

On entering my flat for the first time in three months I felt a mixture of emotions. You'd think I'd have had post-traumatic stress, like when a victim returns to a crime scene yet, I knew there was very little to be scared of. I had nothing to lose; if it was as bad as before I could just go home. But I wasn't going to let those bastards win. If this book was to end with me quitting then surely it wouldn't be a story worth telling?

It was announced that we would have two potential carers who would shadow Nick, Calum and Leo, in order to ultimately make up the other half of the increasingly sparse care team. First to attend was a thirty year old former landscape gardener called Steve, who had been working in a learning disability unit. Laidback and calm he seemed to possess many of the qualities I associated with my carers at home and seemed willing to get to know me and my needs. I recognised the fact that we could enjoy a happy working relationship together when he put me on the toilet for the very first time. Obviously very nervous about the fear of dropping me, when he pulled my boxers down his finger accidently found itself, for a moment, examining the regions of my anal verge. To which Steve stated, "Sorry Josh, I think I just put my finger up your arse." (It's just a shame it wasn't that blonde girl from the first year!) Promptly, we both descended into fits of uncontrollable laughter. This was definitely the ice breaker that we had been looking for, or should I say, 'arse breaker'. The hilarity continued long into the night when we went for a beer at the Student Union, we realised we had a lot in common and more importantly, shared the same bizarre and colourful sense of humour. This was the start of a special working relationship that was to blossom throughout the rest of my university life.

Both Steve and Nick made the perfect team as they understood each other's requirements and how to make it easier for the other to do a good job. I have realised that there's no such thing as a perfect carer, but if I can make up the qualities needed in a care team in order for me to get the most out of life, it's the closest thing to perfect as I'm ever going to get. As a result of spending the best part of fifteen years as a landscape gardener, Steve's back had seen more bad times than Kerry Katona and so it was agreed between the three of us that the physical requirements of the job should be carried out by Nick. Likewise, it could be said that Nick was no Jamie Oliver. So it was agreed that Steve would carry out ninety percent of the cooking duties to make it easier for everyone and to make certain that I wouldn't come down with Salmonella.

During this time the agency eventually found a third carer to complete the new and thriving team in the shape of a twenty-one-year old college graduate, James. As a result of being more my age, it wasn't long before we were able to develop a productive working relationship. Despite already having one existing job as a deputy manager of the Bournemouth branch of Wilkinson, he seemed to understand the flexibility aspect of the job and was very willing to cover as many hours as possible. Also, I was in luck if I ever needed a new toothbrush!

This stability was exactly what I needed to help me concentrate on the second year of university. The second year was where my output really started to ramp up and unlike the first, I knew that my marks for my work would have a direct impact on my overall grade. My first assignment was something new to me: I'd grown up watching what I thought to be some of the finest episode dramas that Britain had to offer, whether it was Heartbeat, Where The Heart Is or Ballykissangel but now I was going to attempt to write one myself. For this we were divided into groups of six with the task of collectively writing a series bible to accompany the drama. A series bible in layman's terms is everything that a writer should know about a series before they put pen to paper. This includes: the overall plot summary, episode outlines and character studies which we all had a hand in devising. Our drama centred around the dramatic happenings in an airport directly following a terrorist attack. Apart from 9/11 I knew nothing about terrorism or airports so felt a little out of my depth. Yet I was definitely up for the challenge!

To conduct the research for such a project we realised that we needed to experience first-hand the everyday running of an airport and we were in a fortunate position to live five minutes from the only domestic airport on the South Coast. With no prior warning, the six of us, plus my carer and university assistant turned up at Bournemouth airport and went straight up to a security guard, where one of us uttered the immortal phrase, "What procedures have you got in place in the event of a terrorist attack?" Well, I have no idea how we all didn't immediately get escorted out of the building. It had only been five years since 9/11 and merely a matter of months since 7/7 and we thought it was a good idea to walk into an airport with no form of ID, no boarding passes, nothing at all really and ask them about terrorism? We must have been mad! Luckily I hadn't grown a beard by that stage!

With our location research over, it was time to write our episodes. We all had to choose one from a possible eight which were included in the series bible that we had just created. I found this process to be the hardest part of my degree because there was a definite criteria that I needed to stick to. As a writer I thrive on the creative freedom of knowing that I can take my work in any direction I choose. This process taught me the discipline of collaborative work and the ability to write something with limitations as opposed to free form imagination. I kept procrastinating until one Sunday evening when Nick and I had nothing to do, all of a sudden I had an idea. We stayed up all night while I dictated and Nick bashed away on the keyboard. Before this the only thing that Nick had scribed for me was insulting text messages to my mates from home, but now he was tasked with scribing a fifty-nine page drama episode. By 2am, tired, drained and emotional, Nick closed my laptop lid as a great feeling of relief came over me. I'd finished it!

This process, however gruelling, was rewarding for the need to collaborate with the drama team and I like to think it made all the members of that team realise that I had just the same experiences to offer as they did. I really wanted to reinforce the fact that, apart from the obvious, I was no different than them and indeed could make relevant contributions just like them. In doing this I think I came over a bit too eager, like I almost had to validate why I was there. Of course at the end of the day, none of that matters as long as we were making progress. Nobody cared about who had what idea or who was talking the most, it was group work and we were all there for the same reason: to get the best grade possible. Therefore our episode drama project was deemed a success and taught me that with the right collaborative dynamics you can achieve a lot.

When it came to the end of term it was agreed that Nick would return to the Isle of Wight with me and provide my personal care at home. By now all the people who helped me out in the past were doing other things and so Nick was the obvious choice. He had done everything for me at Uni so why couldn't he do the same at home? However, on the day when he was due to start on the Island, I received an email informing me that he would no longer be able to work with me.

I was absolutely devastated. It may seem like a cliché, but we had been on a journey together and at that moment there was no one else I needed as much as Nick. I realised that his legacy would be felt for years to come. Unlike many of my previous carers, Nick wasn't trained by any of my immediate family nor had the support of previous carers. So everything he learned was directly influenced by me, thus proving to myself that I could in fact manage my own affairs. To me, a good carer should be able to echo my life, be passionate about the things I'm passionate about, know my life and routines and know how to respond to all key people in my life. Nick was able to do this with the greatest of ease and at that specific moment in time it was difficult for me to imagine how and when I'd get it back.

So I was facing my third year of university without my longest serving carer in Bournemouth. Although I still had Steve, I knew that the successful atmosphere of the second year wouldn't continue. We decided not to renew our contract with the agency and instead Mum and Dad agreed to manage the care themselves which proved successful throughout the rest of my university experience. Around this time my sister's boyfriend Harry and his friend Sam 'Spud', had just graduated from their respective universities. They were looking for work prior to their eventual plan to go travelling for six months. It seemed like a good idea if we could help each other out at this important stage of our lives; I needed two carers to work alongside Steve in order to make up my care team and they wanted to earn money in order to provide for the trip of a lifetime. Also the fact that they were known to me and were from my hometown meant that I would have a link to home that I so needed after the stress of losing probably one of the best carers I ever had.

It was agreed that they should both come and shadow Calum when he was working with me at home in order to obtain an insight. This was a little irrelevant for Harry because he had grown up around me and knew my needs better than most. Because we had socialised a lot together, both of them had no problem in understanding me, so they had already conquered the first hurdle. Harry has always had a great sense of respect. It is natural for him to cater for me without even thinking about it. Empathetic and selfless, Harry was able to identify what was important to me and help me achieve my goals.

Having a lot in common, it wasn't difficult for us to live together for forty-eight hours per week. Both avid Manchester United supporters, I always loved, and still love, catching a game with Harry. Yet one match vividly sticks in my mind; Euro 2008 and the qualifier against Croatia! England needed to beat them by more than two goals to be in with a chance of getting through to the tournament the following summer. Anxious and slightly negative, I sat swearing at the television already admitting defeat before Harry uttered the immortal line, "If we don't win, I'll eat my hat!" Well, for anyone who follows international football you probably remember what happened next. Remember Steve McClaren standing under that massive umbrella looking beaten and forlorn? England were defeated by Croatia which meant we hadn't qualified for Euro 2008. But more importantly than that, Harry was required to eat his hat and I was going to make certain that he remained true to his word! In short, whenever I was with Harry I was always guaranteed a good laugh as he ate pieces of fabric for the sake of his national football team!

Having this familiar support meant that I could dive right into my third-year workload, and what a workload it was! First on my agenda was my dissertation. If you've forgotten the bizarre title of my dissertation it was, A Freudian View of Women in 1970's Sitcom. Instead of reading a substantial amount of Sigmund Freud literature, I thought I would start from entirely the other end of the thesis. So that summer was spent in my bedroom watching hours upon hours of 1970's sitcom and making Harry and Spud write down every single sexual reference which was uttered. It was enough to drive anyone insane even if they did like British sitcom, let alone if they didn't! We must have sat through tens of different types of sitcom before I finally decided upon my main four examples of the genre, which were: Fawlty Towers, The Good Life, Are You Being Served? and Open All Hours. Like so many of my projects, I knew I'd set myself quite a challenge, but I thrive on creative concepts and this was right up my street.

I'm not someone who likes to work to a deadline, I would rather start work at the earliest possible point to ensure I have plenty of time for editing and rewrites. So as soon as I returned to university in September 2007 I just wanted to crack on with it, after all I had decided upon my thesis almost five months previously. This was greatly assisted by Harry and Spud who were used to helping me with research at home and stayed up to date with my progress. With their help my dissertation was completed by Christmas and I could enjoy the holiday without it hanging over my head. Thus proving yet again that with the right support I can accomplish great things!

From the outset, it was clear that Harry and Spud would only work with me for a limited time before their big trip. They finally set a date for their departure in early March, which meant we would be forced to start the whole recruitment process again in order to locate suitable candidates for the role. Around this time, Nick had returned to Bournemouth and was back working under the care agency with a teenage boy. I approached Nick about making a possible return to my care team and as a result of his allocated hours with the teenager it looked very promising. I began looking forward to the prospect of having one of my best carers returning to the fold once again. Yet a few days prior to starting work with me, the care agency informed him that the rotas had changed and he would not be flexible enough to work with me.

It seemed to me that history was repeating itself and yet again there was a hurdle which prevented Nick from working with me. At a similar time Steve informed me that his brother was looking for work in the Bournemouth area and after hearing about my vacant carer job, he was interested to see what it was all about. So it was agreed we would meet over a pint at the Student Union. That evening was filled with laughter and easy conversation and it did not take me long to realise that we would work well together. The following day, I reported back to my parents and sang the praises of Steve's brother, Graham, who preferred to be called Gray. Gray was successful in obtaining the job as my second carer, as easy as that.

Being slightly older than Steve, it didn't take long for me and Gray to realise that our tastes in entertainment were extremely similar. Like me, Gray also has a passion for the glory days of Light Entertainment and it was great to find someone who shared my hobbies. In addition to this, like his brother, Gray is blessed with a bizarre sense of humour which gives mine a run for its money. It was clear we got on well and in time created a successful professional understanding which would outlive the rest of my university experience.

This still left a single vacancy in my care team and with only a few months of my degree to go, I felt like I needed someone who was already a known entity in order to live out the climax of my university experience. For this, I approached James again and told him of my predicament. He had a full time job but agreed to return on a temporary basis. How were we to know that this would turn out to be my university care team for the best part of two years and went a long way to concreting my academic success?

A couple of weeks after James' reappointment, Gray was to tie the knot with his long-term partner before embarking on a two week honeymoon in Turkey. This left a temporary vacancy within the team and I knew wholeheartedly who I wanted to fill this gap. Nick was continuing to work with the teenager just around the corner from the university and by this time Steve had joined the care team in order to fill his working hours when he wasn't with me. I approached Nick about the possibility of him filling in for Gray while he was on honeymoon and to my delight he agreed.

This coincided with the end of my university work load and thus I no longer had educational assistants each day, so my time was my own. It was the perfect climax to my BA as with Nick back at my side it seemed like I had gone full circle.

Towards the end of term it was revealed that my course leader was planning to establish a new Masters course under the umbrella of the media school. I became very interested in such an idea and decided to enrol. However, as stated in previous chapters, a lack of interest during the first year of it being advertised meant that the course would be delayed for a year. I was very willing to wait until the following September, only if my strong and reliable care team would return to support me and luckily for me that is exactly what happened.

After spending a whole year apart, when the team eventually reunited it was like we hadn't been away and my relationship with Steve and Gray grew ever stronger as they were able to provide me with a standard of care which was perfect to suit the university environment. Yet, there was one vital difference. As a result of being away from campus for a whole year, the university had rented my flat to another disabled student with more severe requirements. This meant we were forced to look at alternative accommodation which I was actually excited about. I had always wanted to experience life within the realms of normal accommodation and it looked like this was about to happen.

On visiting a disabled suite at the new university block in the centre of town, I was shocked to learn that I was going to have to be locked in my room at night. I was definitely not going to do that! It was like my worst nightmare. Who else gets locked in a room at night and how can you sleep under such circumstances? I was no prisoner and I knew I wasn't going to settle for it. Fortunately, another option was to move in to a shared house on campus in the middle of the student village. This was the best environment I had been in throughout university as I was finally amongst the action, in the heart of it all, and I loved it! My house mate was a mature student who, luckily, I got on well with and although living with our madness, (Gray and Steve must have taken a lot of getting used to), I think eventually Mark grew to love us.

For the first time I was truly able to experience what university was like for everyone else. I had neighbours who were up for going out and having a good time, I had a social hub which I could bring people back to, and with Mark I had that connection which could make it possible for others to get to know me. Of course this was a brand new experience for Steve and Gray, as they had never worked with me in shared accommodation and it took a while to get used to. Gray would regularly get irate at the neighbours for walking too close to his car and moan about the 'freaky' students which Mark would regularly bring back to the house. But we still knew that this was the perfect atmosphere for me and together Steve and Gray helped me make the most of it. Without their loyalty and consistency throughout the years it would be very hard to envisage my successful progress through my university experience and the emotional attachment that I still hold for Bournemouth. We made the perfect team.

I realise now that it's very difficult to sum up my Uni experience as it threw great contrasts over how I felt about Bournemouth. If, at the start of my BA, you'd have told me that I would have four years at university, I think it would have been enough to send me over the edge. Yet from the support network I developed over those years, it will always occupy a special place in my heart, as I proved to myself and those around me that I could live, work and flourish all on my own. That's a great achievement.

X

Hoist or No Hoist

Twenty-two boxes, twenty-two contestants and only one question… no sorry, wrong programme! This has nothing to do with bankers or Noel Edmonds. Now, one thing I've noticed as a disabled person, people are forever paranoid that you're not getting enough choices like; what you want for lunch, what you want to do with your day, what you want to wear… It goes on and on. In fact, certain people get quite angry if disabled people aren't given the right to make their own choices about everyday life and even spend a lot of their free time campaigning for it. Why? I have no idea. Yet what I find strange, if not verging on surreal, is the unexplained uproar of health care professionals when you tell them that your carer lifts you from place to place. It's like you've just told them that you're a mass murderer or you're in a plot to kill a member of the Royal Family.

The last paragraph I expect may have encouraged you to form an opinion about this issue for yourself. In my experience this is a debate which divides many people and has been known to be as contentious as fox hunting or Brexit! Surely there are a lot more important issues to worry about in the world other than whether a carer is physically capable of lifting someone off the floor or not. It's got absolutely nothing to do with anyone else apart from the carer who is doing the lifting and the person being lifted. That's just my opinion so feel free to shout at the page if you think I'm talking utter nonsense! This is something I feel immensely strongly about and believe that without this choice my life would be very different.

As a child, I was always very small for my age and whilst this was a severe blow to my masculinity and pride, it did have a lot of positives when it came to people being able to move me around and I guess this is still the case for my current care team. Being very slender and unable to reach the all-important five-foot mark by the time I was fifteen put another dent in my masculinity. Yet I was very reassured on a trip to the swimming pool when it was quite apparent that I might not be the tallest but in the 'downstairs department' I am considered to be a giant amongst men. At one point I imagined if you stood my penis up against me it would have been almost the same height. You will be pleased to know it eventually stopped growing otherwise I could be renamed the new Pinocchio, and yes I think it still adjusts in size when I tell lies… or at least that's what I call it! Or if you prefer another analogy, it is like Aladdin's lamp, once rubbed, glitter and a blue figure come out (I still have to visit the doctor about that).

Apart from my genitals, I eventually realised that being little benefited the way people were able to move me… physically and emotionally! Always one of the lads, I found the easiest way to do what my mates were doing was to actually get them to do it with me. When they were old enough to be trusted with taking me out of my wheelchair, there was no limit on what I could do. They were even experienced enough to lend a hand with the physical tasks that my carer Penny began to find difficult. In some way this brought me closer to my friendship circle as I was required to rely on them for many physical tasks which were necessary throughout the school day. It was such a liberation during lunchtime break when either Tom or Kirby would take me for a walk around the common room and more often than not lock me in the tuck shop until I started screaming. Tom in particular went on to become a significant part of my care team and even to this day states that if he hadn't had this grounding at school he may not have thought he would have been able to become my carer in later years.

The ability to be active was a contributing factor which helped me integrate with my peer group. When you're in a wheelchair surrounded by able bodied children it's very important that you are able to have the same physical freedom as everyone else. If they see you kicking a football or attempting to play hopscotch it may increase their confidence in striking up a conversation with you. When they saw me being involved with everything it broke down social barriers and made the other children more inclined to befriend me. During my Primary school days, from the age of five, with Penny's help I was always out of my chair and walking around. I was able to take part in playground games such as football, rounders and the obligatory schoolboy game of 'it'. I may not have been the best player and I'm sure me being on a team was more of a hindrance than a help, but my friends soon became accustomed to the fact that I could almost do anything they could; I would just have four legs instead of two. Penny was the perfect advocate of this and when it came to mixing with new children she had the ability to make my differences irrelevant.

It's a hard thing to get your head around but although I was obviously disabled, I still craved physical activity and everyone around me understood this. They realised I would never be the next Linford Christie but recognised that I needed to get involved in the physical games that everyone else was involved in. It was more about bonding rather than the actual game. I couldn't care less if I won or lost, I just wanted this time with my friends and if I had to get out of my chair to do it, that is what I did.

For someone who spends a large percentage of life in a wheelchair, being able to engage in exercise offers me physical freedom. This feeling has never gone away and even now, when I have been sitting for a considerable length of time, it is an indescribable sensation when someone is physically strong enough to stand me up and take me for a little walk. I can't imagine what it is like for those people in my situation who do not have this luxury.

Apart from the obvious health benefits, exercise put me on a par with my peer group and made it more accessible for them to interact with me. Yet it was agreed that the weekly scheduled session of physical education would not be suitable for me to attend. Instead I was lucky enough to use this time to work with Di. She knew exactly how to gauge these sessions to make them both informative and fun. She recognised that whatever I couldn't do physically, I could make up for with my imagination and the ability to get my thoughts on paper. Therefore, I never thought I was missing out, as whatever I did with Di, was always rooted in fun. However, on reflection, if it could have been organised for me to contribute to a scheduled physical activity, it would have given me that little insight into what the others were doing and I think this would have made my school experience altogether more rounded.

Mum and Dad have always had an amazing sense of foresight. They've spent their whole lives trying to pre-empt the challenges I might face and have always planned to tackle them earlier so that they don't overwhelm me. When I was ten my family up-scaled the family house to a Victorian three storey situated on the main road into Cowes. In order to make it accessible for me, it needed a lot of work doing to it as, just like my Dad, the water works were a bit rusty! Luckily my Dad and Grandad were always very handy. Grandad Barry was a short, portly, old-school electrician who wasn't fazed by anything. Focused, determined and ever- capable. Even at the age of 70 he was still climbing on top of a three-storey house!

It took over two years of blood, sweat and tears from the builders and both my Dad and Granddad to get the house up to a standard that was liveable for the whole family. A large extension on the back of the house was created in order to become both my bedroom and living quarters as I grew up and included a track hoist which was built to take me from my bed into the en-suite bathroom. Although it was a good idea, in the back of my mind I always believed that if someone couldn't lift me, then they shouldn't be doing the job. Not that there's anything wrong with getting hoisted, it's just not my personal preference (I like getting swept off my feet!).

The other positive of the hoist was that my family could assist me in all areas of personal care. But in the end, I found this a bit weird, I mean what other young guy gets one of the family to shower him? I'm used to having male carers who could do everything for me so I don't think it's appropriate anymore. After thirty years I think it's good that my family and I can share a normal relationship. One where I no longer have to rely on them for physical support and we can go about enjoying life together, instead of being forced to rely on them for personal care. Apart from this aspect I am no different to Soph and Lauren and I think that's the way it should be.

While being lifted rather than hoisted is a technique that works for me, I realise that this relaxed attitude to manual handling wouldn't work for everyone. I mean what if I were much bigger and heavier? I never thought about this until I met my very good friend Joe at school. If he could, Joe would stand an astonishing 6ft 3". Growing up he was always big for his age which arguably made it very difficult for someone to move him in the same way as me. However, the ability to have control over his upper body allows him the independence to function much as anyone else. Today Joe is a very accomplished musician and has written several albums of instrumental music and is always gigging around the Isle of Wight and the south coast of England. He hasn't let his disability get in the way of anything and the world is his oyster.

Through spending so much time with Joe in The Den, we actually became quite close and after a while, our friendship blossomed, we soon found ourselves around each other's houses watching a variety of programmes from yesteryear. It was at this time I realised the physical challenges Joe faced which I fortunately was not bound by, due to having capable people to help me. Our relationship has continued, albeit we see each other less frequently due to our busy work schedules.

Spending time with Joe made me realise that every disabled person and their requirements are totally different from each other. Like me, Joe could involve himself in anything he wanted to, providing he had the tools to do it. Just like I needed people to run me around the rec after a football, it wasn't about admitting defeat in activities we couldn't do, it was more about finding a way around it. This involved finding people who were physically strong enough to move him so that we could do anything we wanted to. Why did we have to settle for just watching DVDs and TV when we could do a lot more?

Becoming older and arguably wiser (well, you've probably got something to say about that) has reinforced the safety aspect of me being moved around and I have taken a conscious decision to limit those people who I allow to lift me off the floor. Although I will always be very slight, it remains a big concern of mine and I realise that as I get older I must take the responsibility for my safety and wellbeing. I've realised that there are certain people who move me around better than others and surprisingly this isn't about strength or size, it's more about having an understanding of my body and its capabilities.

Although the ability to move me around without the use of equipment is something I look for in almost all my carers, I realise this element alone is not exclusive in establishing the success of a potential carer. Moreover, if a carer exhibits a specialist skill in a specific field other than the physical aspect of the job; such as an impeccable sense of organisation vital to the development of my creative writing, or skills in homemaking which makes my life increasingly comfortable, then I would make a sacrifice. As with all functioning teams it is important to delegate tasks based on the individual in question and play to their strengths. It would be both unreasonable and a little naive to expect every carer to be able to perform every task with perfect precision.

What I like to refer to as 'the old guard', Stephen and Calum, were able to perfect a method of moving me around which both suited their individual style and meant they did not do any damage to themselves or me. I often hear parents of disabled children saying that, ultimately they do not think of lifting their child as unnatural, as it becomes more of a technique than a physical strain and I would like to think this philosophy was shared by Stephen and Calum. They could do anything with me and still can! Although it is a long time since either Steve or Calum has worked with me on a regular basis, on the rare occasion when they return to the fold, they are still able to move me around like they did all those years ago. They are the Bruce Forsyths of JB Carers! Despite working with a whole host of different carers, I still have an immense amount of trust in these two people and am able to allow them to do almost any physical task with me.

Apart from bathroom activities, Stephen and Calum were the first carers to make moving me into an art form. I use that term very lightly as I recognise it is very much an overused phrase when it comes to all walks of life. However, to me it was an art form as although I am very slight it still requires strength to get me around and it was astonishing just how many activities I could involve myself in thanks to having two capable figures by my side.

The ironic aspect about this professional understanding between myself, Calum and Stephen, was that it was totally devoid of intervention from my parents. I suppose you could say well, why did they need to know? When everyone else reaches a certain age they don't feel the need to relay their personal habits to all and sundry, so why did I? After all, Mum and Dad had fought so hard for me to live a life without limits so this was the ultimate payoff from the great work they had done. I was now independent, I could do anything without the physical help of my family. Just like people who have done the same job for a long time, Steve and Callum adhered to the same techniques every time they worked with me and to the outsider it may have seemed dangerous but to us it was just natural.

Like most aspects of my life, I realised that this understanding would only work if I had likeminded people on board with my own requirements and who were able to distinguish between what was a requirement and what was my preference. Although I like to be moved without a hoist I realise that in certain circumstances this would not be possible. At university, I was bound by legislation which limited what I was able to do, however in terms of my physical stamina, I realised that if I didn't maintain a level of fitness that I would eventually lose my muscle strength.

When I returned home in the summer, after my first year of Uni, I obtained a membership at the local fitness centre in the hope that I would get a stomach like a chopping board and arms like JCBs! People in the gym must've wondered what the hell was going on as I clambered onto the leg extension machine. If only they were playing R Kelly's 'I believe I can fly' as I mounted the equipment!

Initially, the personal trainer did not fully understand my potential in terms of the equipment I could use. He probably thought that I was surgically stuck to my wheelchair. Therefore, my introductory three months was spent solely on the cable machine, which I am able to control from the confines of my wheelchair. It wasn't until I started to enquire about the other equipment that he realised there was more

(From left) Jo Tyler. John Foster, Mike Dixon, Dick Fiddy, Colin Edmonds and Russel Biles at Following the money launch

(From left) Sally (Harrys mum) my mum, Sophie, me and Harry

Charity Show in aid of Todd

My Family

Lauren (top left), Penny (top right), Sophie (bottom left) and Di (bottom right)

Lauren, Me & Dad

Me & Andy

With the family at Bestival

Me & Sophie at the Brits!

With Steve Barnes, my carer

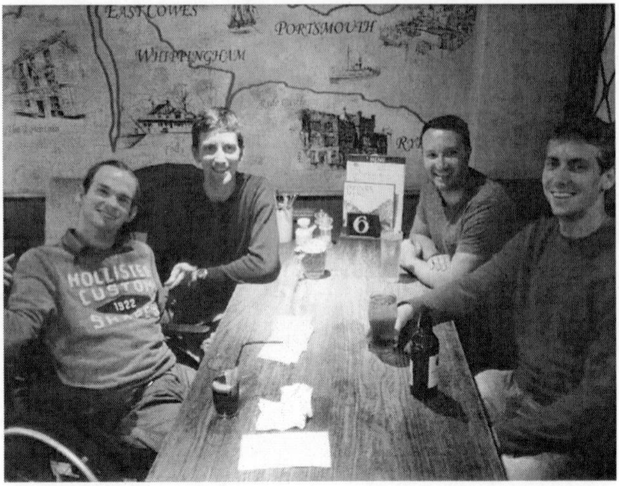

Me and Tom (top left), Stew (Top right) and Sam (bottom right)

Me & Tom at Cowes Week

With Barry Cryer

Me & Graham Thorne

Me and James

The "Crip Climb" – group pic

scope to explore in terms of my routine. From then on, I began a weekly schedule on a range of different equipment including- leg extensions, pec flys, lat pull down, etc. God, writing it down makes myself sound actually pretty fit, if you want a calendar, I'll give you my address at the end (that was a joke for all you stalkers out there!). This is where I find it important to have people who can confidently move me and if they can't, it creates a problem. This is the ultimate test and I've actually had carers get really pissed off if they can't do it…

This meant that if I was at the gym with a carer who was not overly physical, the personal trainer (or affectionately named Love Muscle) would lift me on and off the equipment himself. I was comfortable with him moving me as a result of being in this environment he was used to lifting heavy weights, so lifting me was like handling a bag of sugar! This expanded the pool of carers who were able to accompany me and meant that I could always attend a gym session every week, irrespective of which carer I had working with me.

During my gap year, we employed a history graduate who exhibited a flare for creative writing and was my intellectual equal. Yet Tom's slight stature meant that he was unable to participate in the physical tasks which by now I had grown accustomed to with my other carers. Therefore, figures such as 'the Love Muscle' became increasingly significant in order for me to continue doing the things that I had the desire to do. I guess it made me realise, not for the first time, how lucky I was to obtain carers who are able to lift me.

When I returned to university in September 2009, I was determined to maintain a considerable level of fitness and realised this would only be possible if I was lucky enough to encounter a figure like the "Love Muscle". This was of even greater importance as a result of the physical capabilities (or lack thereof) of Steve and Gray. Yet my fears were removed when I realised that the gym manager was a friend from my first year. My mate Ian, agreed to provide me with personal assistance every Thursday night where I could access the equipment and stretch, which was vital to maintaining a level of flexibility. This soon included Ian being able to take me out of my wheelchair and walking me around the gym corridor at the end of each session. This was successful until one evening I got stuck in between a pair of locked automatic doors. What were we to do? My wheelchair was on the other side of the door and we had no way of getting back. Ian laid me on the floor and went round to open the door but things got even funnier when the 90's Pilates class ended and women crowded out to find me lying on the floor! I have no idea what they thought!

My hour long gym session with Ian, proved to be the only event where I was able to easily enjoy a sense of physical freedom, away from the strict confines of my wheelchair. I knew that every Thursday at 7 o'clock I would be able to move and stretch as much as I wanted. When I'm working up to 8 hours a day my muscles can get very tight and it was so nice when I could stand up, stretch and go for a walk. Every time I lose a carer I wholeheartedly trust, I always assume that my physical freedom will be forced to stop and I'll never get it back. This is one of the biggest concerns affecting my life to date and I'm still scared that I'll wake up one day and everything will stop; no more walking, no more getting out my chair, I'll just be a slave to my hoist

Apart from people like Nick and Ian, I didn't really stop and think about the importance of my physical fitness at Uni. There was so much else going on, that I didn't have time. University is a unique setting where you are forced to make sacrifices. In the case of my life, those sacrifices I was forced to forgo outweighed the incredible experiences and the emotional (dare I say it) journey which I found myself on. I suppose in a perfect world I would have liked to have been a little more active during the latter years of my university time, yet I would not have wanted to give up the good times spent with carers Steve and Gray, for that I am most thankful. In the words of Elton John, it was, “No sacrifice”!

On my return home during the autumn of 2010, I became resigned to the fact that my days of enjoying a substantial physical lifestyle may have been over. I returned to a whole new care team which I did not know or have any emotional attachment to. To top this off my membership at the gym had expired and by then the “Love Muscle” had moved on to pastures new, ironically in Bournemouth! Yet my fears were unfounded when we appointed James Hudson, a nineteen year old college graduate who had just moved to the island to be with his girlfriend.

It is always a difficult subject to approach when training a new carer. Yet, I always remain very curious to establish if they are in fact going to be a 'lifter'. James is average height at five-foot seven-inches and still exhibits childlike features. At first I thought this would be a similar situation to my other lightweight carers, very willing but not that able. After spending a day in Bournemouth with Gray and a day with my former helper Stephen, he was ready for his first day alone and then I thought this was the perfect opportunity to pop the question, ‘hoist or no hoist?’ to which he replied, ‘What would you prefer?’ I recommended that he sat me on the sofa and tried to lift me off. At this point we would find out if it would be possible for him to work without a hoist. He did so and I felt as safe as if Calum or Stephen had done it. Ever since that day James has never needed assistance from a hoist.

It was soon realised that myself and James shared the same attitude when it came to the physical elements. Once again, I could involve myself in physical activities without need of an external source to aid me. For something that I disregarded as a forgotten luxury at university, it had stirred something within me which reminded me of how important physicality was to all aspects of my life. It just took a capable helper such as James to teach me that once again, I could do anything. Despite being of small stature, James is capable of moving me however I want and wherever I want. Here was a gym junkie who was also on my wavelength, so I had the best of both worlds. James could now help facilitate all areas of my life and has rightfully secured the nickname 'Big Guns'.

The decision to move into my own home in December 2011 reinforced my determination to re-establish a sense of mobility into my life. This was my own home and I could live by my own rules and by this time the new recruit George Gard, thankfully shared the same attitude. This was the life I wanted and I realised in terms of my physical freedom, the sky was the limit. My days of waiting for Calum to make a special appearance and walk me around the garden were over.

Over the years I have remained very mindful of my battle with those who I deem fit to move me. It wasn't until I was in my late 20's that I met my carer Ben and it changed my perception of my physical limitations all over again. It's always very difficult when training new carers as to what I need from my physical life. However like James, Ben was able to identify with the importance of me maintaining fitness and well-being and it wasn't long before I felt comfortable with Ben doing anything with me.

After a lifetime of debating and arguing with different people about the manner in which I wish to be handled, I have resigned myself to the fact that there will always be controversy over the way an individual moves me from place to place. Throughout the care sector it is obvious that lifting is considered to be outlawed. However, I believe this is all bullshit. You can't stop people living how they want to, so I think more people should be asked that all important question, "Hoist or no hoist?"

XI

The "Crip Climb"

Not starting with a sarky opener for this one, it's pretty much what it says on the tin! In fact, this chapter is totally different to what has gone before and nothing to do with carers, disability or entertainment. In 2018 I decided to take on a different sort of challenge. One that would totally take me out of my comfort zone. After all, tapping away on my iPad and talking to agents of the stars day after day does get a little tedious sometimes. (What am I saying? It doesn't get tedious… it's great... am I arguing with myself again?)

I've never really been one for physical challenges. Funny that… I've always thought they were for people with far better physical prowess than me. Yet last year, at a dinner party in my friend Sarah's house, she told me of her upcoming mountain walk in the Brecon Beacons National Park. For those that may not know, the Brecon Beacons is in South Wales and is a challenging range of mountains. So challenging that the British Special Air Service use it for their selection process. So it isn't a 'walk in the park'.

Having never even gone to Brecon I was just interested to know what it was like. We got talking and a while later

Sarah said, "Have you ever thought about hiking a mountain Josh?" The simple answer to that question was, "No!" I can't even walk to the toilet, let alone up a bloody mountain - the only mountains I'd previously thought about were Cold or Big! (For those of you who are up on your 1990's one-hit-wonders!). Yet it did get me thinking… Could I actually get to the top of one?

Anyone who knows me is well aware that despite my strong opinions about the way I like to be moved, I also have fears about who it is who moves me. Jesus, if you catch me on a bad day I won't let anyone move me, let alone a whole team! So I knew that if I was actually going to do this, it was going to have to be with the right people and that I would have to put an enormous amount of trust in whoever I selected (yeah, I know I sound like a diva... yet again!). I decided, quite quickly if I'm honest, that yes! I would try to climb a mountain.

So I needed to assemble a team of unfortunate souls who would assist me to get up this large hill! It was like assembling The Avengers - I knew exactly the team I wanted and was absolutely overwhelmed when everyone accepted! I've always struggled to know what people think of me, even those closest to me and this gesture was enough to make me believe that people do care about me and want to see me succeed. I was going to climb Pen y Fan! Again, for those of you (like me!) who might not be familiar with the area, Pen y Fan is the highest peak in the Brecon Beacons National Park, at 886 metres above sea-level. What on earth had I let myself in for?

In a funny sort of way, I think 'walking me' requires a far better technique than lifting me, because you need to be totally in sync with my body and the way it moves. I need to know that the person walking me is going to let me walk at my pace and in the style I like. I've lost count of how many times new carers automatically assume that I don't actually walk at all. They seem to think I just like to be held in a way that looks like I'm walking, but really my legs are only dangling and taking less weight than a gust of air. This couldn't be further from the truth. I like to think I can take my own weight and merely need support for my top half for balance. It takes a toll though. Forget leg day at the gym, walking takes all my energy so, to me, it's clearly obvious that I'm actually doing something.

Obviously, if I wanted to do this challenge I needed to start putting some training in. For eight months I slowly increased my walking regime in a bid to give me the slightest chance of completing such a mission. My team and I were out in all weathers experimenting with different terrains and different walking techniques to prepare me for the big day. For someone who spends 90% of their waking hours in a wheelchair, it's very refreshing to see the world from another perspective, i.e. upright, as opposed to sat down. It's at these times that I realise I am very lucky to have this luxury and I do have real sympathy for those in a similar situation to myself who don't have the opportunity to stand up. There are many with CP who I'm sure would love the opportunity to walk up a mountain, but either lack the physical or economic resources to do it. In this aspect I think you could say I'm very lucky. I'm certainly not the only person with CP to crave physical stimulation and I certainly can't imagine a life without it.

Compiling my perfect walking team was a difficult process. I not only had to consider people's physical strength but also their technique in walking me. Like anything, everyone has their own way of handling me which is perfectly fine, but I have preferred ways that I like to walk. I needed to make sure that the people in the team were going to respect my preferences. It took several months, but I eventually settled on one of my best friends, Tom, my carer Ben, his brother Sam, and friends Sam and Frank, with moral support from a large group of my friends who were absolutely vital to me completing the challenge.

I always knew that conquering a mountain was going to require hard work, dedication and a lot of training. It was a long time since the days of the 'Love Muscle' and Ian at uni. Despite renewing my membership when I first came back from uni, what with my projects such as 'Following The Money' and 'Beyond The Title' I somehow fell out of love with the gym and I could tell that my body was suffering as a result. I started by enrolling at my local fitness centre.

To see me bounding into the gym and heading straight to the leg extension, I imagine is very disconcerting for some people – rather like a blind person playing snap. Yet the gym was useful to increase my core strength and fitness as I might have been lean but I was so unfit! After doing my regular routine of leg extensions, lat pull down and sit-ups, we realised that there was scope to actually do walking training at the gym. This was where I really started to test myself and despite being a totally different terrain to a mountain, it allowed me to see how far I could actually walk, which at first wasn't that far and not that impressive! The benefit of being in the gym meant that I could slowly build up distances in my own time and at my own pace. With Ben's support, I went from walking half a mile in one hour to two miles in one hour in just two to three weeks. I think that's what you call progress!

We then expanded outside of the gym routine to experiment with different terrains and were frequently out in all weathers walking a whole range of distances. To give me experience with walking an incline we used the downs on the Island. Ben was the perfect person to do this with me as he understood the way I preferred to be walked and could do it for a long period of time. Although it was training, it was also a great feeling to be active and get the feeling of wind in my hair. For me, nothing is greater than the feeling of being upright and having the ability to move freely. Yet could I do that for a prolonged period of time? This is where it really hit home what I'd actually let myself in for and suddenly I was experiencing little niggles and injuries in my right hip and lower back.

My walking technique consists of someone supporting my upper body by wrapping their arms under mine and making sure that my head remains over my feet at all times. It ensures my core is upright and my centre of gravity and balance are in equilibrium. This may be a rather obvious thing to the able bodied amongst us, but for me who is at the mercy of whoever is walking me, it becomes a lot more complex. As a consequence, we discovered that my left leg would flick out when I took a step, which resulted in me having substantial pain in my hip flexors. This was not going to defeat me and so I enlisted the help of a sports massage therapist to ease the pain. Like most therapies, it actually increased the pain temporarily, but soon the magic worked and I was ready to conquer Pen y Fan!

Yet disaster was about to strike as just a month before the big day, my carer Ben suffered a major injury to his arm and shoulder leaving my challenge hanging by a thread. I still realised that I'd have the support of the whole team but without Ben I knew I wouldn't have that safety net which I needed to get me to the top. His walking technique was absolutely perfect and I had to find someone else who was able to replicate it.

Luckily, I have some great friends and when I told one of them, my old friend Dom, of my predicament he instantly offered his services. I can't begin to tell you how relieved I was to have him on board. Dom is just one of many friends who would go to the ends of the earth to help me out and I feel so genuinely grateful to have this support. Over the years, Dom has helped me conquer many things and one memory stands out quite vividly; around my 17th birthday my friends were beginning to have their first driving lessons and I began to feel down about my own limitations. This was just another rite of passage that I could not be involved in. Then Dom had an idea: he drove me to an empty car park (no, we weren't going dogging!) where he sat me on his lap and allowed me to steer the car. In a funny sort of way, this made me feel like I was getting the same experiences as everyone else. Dom has always believed that I can do anything that I put my mind to and he was the perfect person to help me with the challenge of Pen y Fan.

Our friend Sarah had been campaigning for the charity 'Brainwave' and I felt I wanted to do the same. It's a great feeling when you know that you are raising money for a worthwhile cause and the charity helps so many children who are affected with life changing brain injuries, so I felt it was relevant. Over the next three months myself and Ben arranged some quizzes and established a formidable social media campaign. I was encouraged by the news that even before we began our great ascent we had hit our target of £1000 for Brainwave. This was absolutely amazing and so I was fairly relaxed, happy and looking forward to a 'gentle stroll' to the highest peak in the Brecons!

On the morning of Saturday 5th May 2018, I found myself at the base of the mountain surrounded by fifteen of my closest friends in preparation for my biggest challenge to date. There were people everywhere and it seemed that Pen y Fan is a well walked trail for anyone and everyone, irrespective of age or ability. This settled any remaining nerves I may have had and as the team congregated at the picturesque base I was reminded that I was among some of my favourite people in the world. Even though it was gonna be tough I was definitely in perfect company.

The walk began with Tom at the helm. He's really confident in moving me around and therefore had no issue in helping me find the perfect pace. As we walked I was able to take in the beauty that surrounds this well-trodden mountain range. I felt fit and ready and I just hoped it would last! Tom has been walking me for years and it's become almost second nature for him to move me, so I knew he wouldn't have a problem. In fact we realised that we had walked fifty metres without breaking sweat and it was frankly time for someone else to have a go. Next up was Frank, he'd been my carer in the past so everyone assumed that they could leave him to it, but he found it difficult to recreate the technique. Yet Frank is not a quitter and was determined to play an active role in getting me to the top. With a little help from Ben, Frank was able to perfect his technique and gradually grasped what was required.

Wondering if I was making it too hard for everyone, this was the only point during the whole challenge where I considered giving up, but giving up has never been, or never will be, an option for me. Not through school, university or my career, so why would I give up on a physical challenge? After all, I had fought so hard to maintain my physical independence and I felt this was the ultimate acknowledgement that I had conquered the ability to remain active throughout my twenties and into my thirties. Something that was difficult to imagine at several stages of my life. On top of that, Frank wasn't quitting, so why would I?

One of the hardest things was knowing when and equally important, when not, to take a break. I didn't want to rest for too long and risk not being able to get back up again, yet I knew that if I pushed myself too much I would ultimately do more harm than good. So, I was very methodical about when I took breaks and only rested until I got my breath back. This gave me a fresh energy to conquer the next stage of the walk. With these short breaks I was able to get into a stride which I felt was manageable and it maintained my heart rate at a healthy beat. Even though Tom, Dom and company perfected a great rhythm, there were just a handful of times when I really needed Ben to jump in and see me through harsh terrain. Although instructed by his osteopath that under no circumstances should he attempt to walk me, at these critical times Ben realised that if he didn't step in there was no way I would complete it. So, he sacrificed jeopardising his own health just to help me achieve my goal... something that I'll never forget!

After walking several metres with Ben, I would realise that I was back in the zone and be ready for someone else to take the reins once again. Dom continued to get me into a nice rhythm which was combined with the news that we were now over halfway. The path slowly changed from smooth concrete to uneven flint, something which I hadn't accounted for in my training and suddenly I needed to be extra aware of my foot placement to avoid rolling an ankle. At that point it was agreed that I should wear an ankle splint as a precaution. I'd never worn any sort of splint before and was unsure how I would get on with it, yet as soon as Ben put it on I realised that it was going to be a great help. It kept my ankle straight so that I could concentrate on walking rather than merely avoiding injury. The last thing I needed was my ankle going the same way as my hip had in training!

Strapped up and ready to go again, my thoughts turned to the reason we were doing this. Brainwave is a charity which supports children with mental and physical disabilities, including their families, throughout the UK. Our friend Sarah had already raised a fair amount of money for them before returning to her native Australia and we wanted to carry on her tradition. Also, if a charity such as Brainwave had been around when I was younger, I most certainly would have taken advantage of the resources they have to offer. In a funny sort of way raising money for them seemed the right thing to do. Yet apart from that charity, I needed a good incentive to get me to the top and thinking of people who are tragically no longer with us was just the emotional determination that I needed. Alice Turner had been part of my early years' development team and had a dominant hand in getting me into mainstream education. Sadly she passed away in early 2016 leaving a whole string of disability success stories in her wake. I felt this was a fitting tribute to her memory and legacy and was just hoping that I could do her proud!

Forcing myself to set the emotional incentives of the challenge aside for a moment, I was faced with one of the steepest parts of Pen y Fan. Nearing the end of the trail, the gradient became a lot more gruelling. Originally the consensus of the group was that I should be carried up this part but Tom had other ideas. Tom has always had a lot of faith in my physical ability and this was arguably putting it to the ultimate test. Not even allowing me to stop for a break, Tom knew that if I didn't just keep going and work through the pain, I would never reach the summit. At that precise moment I thought Tom was such a Sergeant Major! How dare he push me to my physical limits like this? Yet when he eventually let me stop and I could see the top in the distance, I realised that the hard work was paying off. Tom just knew I needed a bit of tough love to get me through!

After well over two miles, I was on the home stretch and Dom was the unfortunate one to do the last stint. Tired, in pain and frankly in need of a stiff drink, I could almost smell the finish line (or was it my B.O?!). I began to imagine what it would look like: I was told that it would be a pile of stones shaped into a tower (or a cairn to use the proper name). Yet what people didn't tell me was that there are quite a few stone-shaped towers near the top of Pen y Fan and every time I saw one I thought I was done... but no, I just had that bit extra to go. I began to get transfixed on stone-shaped artefacts until I realised the massive gradient above me was leading to the official peak. I sure as shit wasn't going to fail now, not this close to the end.

I felt I could hear the Rocky soundtrack inside my head as I clambered up with Dom who was by now doing most of the work. Suddenly I heard lots of people chanting my name. Was I in heaven? No, I was at the top of Pen y Fan and just about to touch the monument!

What a feeling! A whole range of emotions raced through my head accompanied by exhaustion, relief and mostly, a lorry load of pride. After spending my whole life battling to remain physically fit and able, making all those physical sacrifices at Uni for the sake of my education, finally I had conquered a feat of endurance. I truly loved the ecstasy of being there at the top, feeling so happy to be there. When I was reunited with my wheelchair I remember taking a moment to let it sink in and to look out at the amazing view. I'd been walking for over two and a half hours and despite the aches and pains in my legs, it felt amazing! Not in my wildest dreams (and believe me, I have some quite elaborate ones!) did I think I would ever get to the top of a mountain let alone walk up one. Yet I had done it, I had conquered Pen y Fan!

For someone who hadn't even considered undertaking a physical challenge of any magnitude, it was so exhilarating to stand at the top and look back on what I'd accomplished. I never thought it would even be possible but with the support of the best friends a man could possibly have, I had done it! Without the amazing team around me I would never have been where I was and whilst it's very easy for me to get the plaudits, the team behind me were the real heroes. They made the impossible seem not only possible, but within my reach. It's quite clear that I have some of the very best friends anyone could wish for and for that, I am extremely thankful.

Climbing Pen y Fan wasn't just a physical challenge, it was the ultimate proof that with the right support and encouragement, a bit of grit and determination, I can accomplish anything and I just can't wait to see what challenge awaits me next.

XII

Adapted

So my friends, we have reached the final chapter. You are on the home stretch! In concluding this book, I realise that it's not only the reader who has been on a journey of discovery. It's been extremely cathartic for me to relive and analyse the major components which have contributed to making me the man I am today. When I began the preparation for this project I imagined that I would be telling the story of a disabled man and his quest to become accepted into the mainstream. I somehow believed that I had to prove something about my attitude towards disability and almost justify my thought processes about my own life. Yet, from writing it, I can see that it doesn't matter a toss.

That is not to say that after writing a whole book on my attitude towards disability, I should somehow disregard my own perception of my condition. I am still very proud of the way I look at my disability, not in an egotistical, arrogant way but it's a lot easier than being uncomfortable with it. By writing this book, people with disabilities might think, 'Oh yeah, I feel like that,' or, 'What is he on about?' But if you can relate to any of the points I've made and/or you have experienced what I have, then maybe you feel that you can air your own feelings about the way you are. Surely this is only a very positive thing and if I can be the figurehead of this minor social rebellion, then just call me Johnny Rotten!

Even from a very young age I realised that in order to contribute to everyday life I was required to adapt myself. The earliest memory I have of this was when I played the part of the "Bethlehem Taxi" in the playschool nativity, aged five. I don't recall much of my performance but just remember being watched by people in the room and knowing their reaction to me was very different to that of Mary and Joseph. Gran often told me that she felt proud that I was able to use my disability in a positive way and when I looked at her with a smile she burst into tears. In her words, "I had done it".

Yet it would take a lot more than a bit part in a children's nativity to prove to myself that I had done 'it'. This being if I ever work out in fact what 'it' is. Unfortunately, my Gran is no longer around for me to ask her what her definition of 'it' was. However, I can offer my idea of a definition: Celebrating and understanding one's condition, with the desire to create and adapt upon your given lifestyle in order to contribute and live alongside your contemporaries. Yeah, I know what you're thinking, a lot of big words to sum up those two simple letters, but I hope you see what I'm getting at.

Even in that playschool, at that very tender stage of my life, I still recognised the need to feel part of a group which helped me shape my identity. It was clear that my disability was something that would be impossible to ignore. Yet, by the way I was treated by influential adults and my feeling of acceptance into any group, I was able to make my disability both hidden and more importantly, irrelevant. That doesn't mean it could not be celebrated on occasions when it was suitable for me to offer my peers an insight into what it was like to live with Cerebral Palsy. In those situations my disability was never ignored but put to a positive use in changing other's perception of me. As I grew up and became acclimatised to the adult world, I guess it became a very useful ongoing social technique.

There have been many instances in my life where I have needed to change peoples' perception of disability in order to achieve my potential (for God's sake, I have gone on about it long enough in this book) yet I think you would be surprised to learn my opinion of what has been the most important step to changing people's perception of me. Before I moved out in December 2011, Mum and Dad assumed that we would roll around in our big Victorian house until the stage where they would require more personal care than I did. But now, I feel like all members of the family are on a level playing field and we can enjoy a normal relationship away from the carer/client one, which we may have slipped into had I still been living in the family home. For me, this is a great feeling of freedom and for my parents I guess it's a realisation of the natural path of their youngest and most precious cargo.

It is only when putting this story down on paper that I realise the direction and trail which my life has been forced to take in order to achieve my personal goals. This dates back to my very first day at Northwood Primary where it was realised by all the significant players in my story that whilst I would be able to attend almost all of the obligatory timetable, there would need to be some adaptations in place in order to cater for my individual needs. But it's the way it was done that I think is so remarkable; Di would never make it look like I was doing anything different to the rest of my peers. In fact you could argue I wasn't! It was more making the most of the school day and playing on the things I could do instead of worrying about the things that I couldn't. So, I always knew that I wasn't an average pupil who could take part in all realms of the mainstream timetable but instead it was adapted. Granted, I loved having the sessions with Di, but why adapted? Why does my life always have to be a little bit different from the common man? Why can't I just make do with mainstream concepts? I don't have the answers. But from reading this book I hope that you realise the importance of me needing to ask these questions.

Throughout earlier chapters I did speak of specific carers such as Steve and Calum who would break down the barriers of social interaction between myself and my friendship group. I have never established in my own mind if this was in fact being accepted into a mainstream social situation, as it still involved intervention from a third party in order to adapt something which was relatively standard. Adapting to my surroundings and involving myself in any given activity has been the key to forging friendships with people who would not otherwise had the confidence or inclination to befriend me. This is only possible providing I have a capable figure by my side and whilst this technique proved successful in my younger days, I feel one has to update this technique in order to breakdown social barriers in the adult world.

I often hear interviews with accomplished entertainers who all state that the need to create a character of themselves for the screen is vital to make the obvious differentiation between work and home life. In a way this is the method I use when meeting new people. I realise conversation will prove a lot harder than they may be used to and if I can create a heightened image of myself it will put the listener at ease and aid with any embarrassing, awkward silences brought on by miscommunication. This is both a proven method of allowing people to see the real person in the wheelchair and another example of how I have been forced to adapt myself in order to achieve acceptance. Such a device will hopefully go some way to assisting me in both future social and professional situations where I find myself being forced to interact with a whole range of different people. If I hit the big time, at least I will have already created an alter ego which will be both endearing and appealing to a mass audience.

The downside of this technique means that it is very difficult for people to get to know me quickly as both parties are required to break down social barriers and become a little more comfortable. But again, I am very adamant for people to know the real me and if I can indeed make this process both quick and more effective, then this is what I do. As stated in previous chapters this is only possible when I am aided by a familiar face who can help with interaction and reduce the awkwardness of the situation. Yet why does it have to be like this? Why do I need to rely on that third party? If I wanted to interact with someone via an external method, I would have sent them an email.

A common misconception about my difficulties in communication is that the listener somehow thinks that I will become increasingly irritated and frustrated if I am not instantly understood. In conversation with my former primary school head teacher, as part of my research for this book, she recalled a particular time when Penny was on a break. I attempted to strike up a conversation with my teacher to which she instantly became fearful at the thought of either me having chronic diarrhoea, a life-threatening illness or a raging thirst. When Penny returned the teacher was baffled to discover that I only wanted to know if she saw Cilla Black on Blind Date on Saturday night. I agree you couldn't blame her for not understanding, due to the randomness of my conversation but I guess this was the first time that I found myself being forced to attempt to make myself understood to an unfamiliar audience.

Even to this day I am still adamant that I will be able to engage in conversation even when my audience may not be overly familiar with understanding me. I believe this is the only solution to bridging the gap between myself and the average person. Sceptics of this method often accuse me of putting relative strangers in a very uncomfortable situation where they have no idea what to do. Yet if I am able to remain calm and patient with them and make light of the situation, my audience will be more likely to pick up the thread of my utterances as opposed to me becoming increasingly panicked. Panic would only serve to make my speech even more difficult to understand. Hopefully this technique reduces the embarrassment brought on by misunderstanding and extends the pool of people who would actually enter into conversation with me.

As the title of this book suggests I have adapted my life to be part of the mainstream. However in this instance it is not always me who needs to adapt for other people. Before people are prepared to engage in conversation with someone like me, they need to overcome their own prejudices and become aware of the social requirements of the disabled person they wish to interact with. It sounds like a very difficult concept but if you are prepared for the fact that it may take a little longer to converse with them, it may not be that bad. It's like riding a bike, you just have to give it a go and once you have bitten the bullet you find it increasingly easier.

Communication is not the only barrier which I am forced to overcome when interacting with the general public. As a result of my Athetoid Cerebral Palsy, my unwanted movement sometimes is just that and occasionally, I do resemble a skeleton on a rollercoaster dancing to 'You Should be Dancing' by the Bee Gees. For someone who is not aware that I am mentally and psychologically sound they would be excused for thinking that I am merely a shell of a human being with (like my hairline) not much going on up top! However, people who know me best might argue the previous statement of self-proclaimed mental fortitude. Yet how can we as a nation change this stereotype? Does it need changing at all? The British are often criticised in coming over as too polite, so if this is the case perhaps we are too scared to find out.

Before this subject starts to resemble some sort of a crusade about attitudes towards disability in the public eye, let me assure you that I am not attempting to bring about social change with this book. Oh God, I'm not one of those infuriating disabled rights campaigners who gets beside themselves when there's no lift at a railway station! I am merely airing my perception of different attitudes towards someone with my condition and the changes in acceptance over time. Hopefully this is an aspect of disability which will only ever improve by the wide ranging attitude of citizens who now call Britain home.

However, this is not something that either bothers or affects me on a daily basis. It really is only on rare occasions that I think of myself within this disabled demographic and do not feel the need to identify myself with this specific social group. Like anyone, if you hear good news about something in your area that you'd like to do, it's a great feeling. For example, when my local music festival announces that they are building an initiative to ensure their facilities are accessible for a broad range of disabled people, it makes me not just excited for myself but I recognise the fact that so many other people in my situation will be able to have this experience.

This subtle change in the attitude towards inclusion and equality within many social arenas, is surely only a very positive step towards disabled people being accepted into society. If I can benefit from adaptions such as the rise of wheelchair access, complementary carer tickets, disabled friendly hotel rooms and wheelchair taxis to name but a few, they will go some way towards making my life both easier and more efficient. But I do not view these issues as part of my social make up. They are just issues that I am forced to confront on a daily basis. Undeniably I would struggle to live a comfortable life without them, but that doesn't mean they should form the backbone of my views and opinions.

It is only in certain situations that I am forced to realise that I am in a small minority of an ever growing population.

To the outside world I am a mere name on a disabled guest list and frankly a vulnerable adult who requires assistance from other people. In this instance, why should I decide to deem it necessary to rebel against the special treatment which my disability occasionally offers me? If I should see a beautiful woman standing next to me it is good to know that I can have a little touch and then blame it on a sudden spasm (that is a joke…). As you can see, there are a lot of positives in giving in to the special awareness that the consensus has of disability and as the old saying goes, 'If you've got it, flaunt it!'

This is another example of my continuous desire for social adaption as I understand that the public in general have very fixed concepts regarding disability. Irrespective of my discussion throughout earlier chapters about changing people's perceptions, I appreciate that in certain situations I am required to go along with the prejudices that some members of society continue to uphold regarding people like me. Although I do not necessarily agree with these misconceptions, it is far easier to repress my feelings rather than challenge people on what they believe is the right approach to take. I believe that so long as people like me are aware of these misconceptions, there is no reason why it would be wrong to attempt social interaction. Why should we be any different from anyone else?

Yet on a positive note, by and large I am very proud of the way I have overcome social interaction difficulties and believe it is one of my greatest achievements to date. The key to this success has been both to understand and appreciate the requirements of my listener/audience. Just like the general public, my listener may have strong preconceptions about what it is to interact with a disabled person. In order to bridge the gap between myself and my listener, I feel compelled to do all I can to make them feel at ease and attempt to make the interaction as natural as possible. This becomes easier when I am able to gauge the competency of the listener and how comfortable they are in the situation.

The satisfaction for me arises when I am able to find a method of making myself understood to a relative stranger and find a successful method which puts both parties at ease.

The breakthrough in my communication method is another explanation as to why I get increasingly irritated by staring onlookers in the street. Closely followed by my annoyance at elderly women who walk over to me and stroke my head accompanied by the expression, "Bless him." If I can conquer the art of social interaction with people of my own age, why do I still find it appropriate to smile and accept the severe prejudices which the older generation still uphold? This image of disabled people which continues to stick in the mind of many members of the old guard is not only wrong, but totally inappropriate for the inclusive society which we pride ourselves on being. My forehead unfortunately is not big enough for me to write my whole life story on (as you can see from reading this book) and if it was why should I find it necessary to explain my life to a stranger in order to obtain social acceptance? Maybe this book will hopefully answer some of the burning questions which the public are very interested to know and in time as a result of increasing awareness of diversity, they may not deem it necessary to approach people like me.

Fortunately, all of the significant figures within my life assist me in rebelling against the fixed concepts which some continue to uphold. This is something that I rarely think about and I guess I sometimes take for granted. All of my family and friends accept my disability and make adaptations themselves in order for me to become involved with general life. Like me, I guess they never really stop to analyse what impact these adaptations have on their own lives and how natural it can become to do this without giving any of it much thought. If my family did not all share this accommodating outlook, my life would be very different and perhaps I would never have achieved my academic or social potential. This attitude has spurred me on to better myself throughout all areas of my life and has given me the tools and techniques required to cope in the independent world.

Together with my reliable support network and my ability to overcome the many challenges of life, I would say that I have achieved a lot over the last thirty years and have relished in finding outlets for my talents. I have been able to make my disability irrelevant to the creative contribution that I am able to make. Apart from writing this book, it is my ambition to become a screenwriter for television, which arguably my disability will not have any part to play in. I would like for my work to be accepted on its own merit, rather than being known as written by a disabled writer. The subject matter is not likely to echo issues of disability or diversity so personally it would be inappropriate for me to disclose my disability at such an early stage. So why is it even relevant?

If the situation ever arose where I was indeed lucky enough to become successful in the world of television screenwriting, I would like to think that when I actually revealed to the industry I was disabled, it would receive an underwhelming reception. No special treatment. No patronising pats on the back, or well-wishers saying, "You should be very proud of yourself, you're a true inspiration." Not even an acknowledgement of my disability. If I was successful in the art of screenwriting, I would have obtained success through the quality of my art, not my disability. So in this instance my disability would not have any impact on my professional life whatsoever. Yet it is difficult to know whether my career as an interviewer has been impacted by people's first impression of me and I acknowledge that some of my subjects may be more inclined to agree to an interview just because I'm disabled. This is something that is totally out of my control and if this is the case, I have to take the opportunity and go along with it. I just hope that when people meet me they realise that despite my limitations I'm just like any other media professional.

You may be thinking that this attitude is a substantial disservice to the many achievements discussed in this book and that I should be proud of how I haven't allowed my disability to get the better of me. However, in my own mind I feel that as a person I have a lot more to do in order to feel a sense of achievement. Despite the many hurdles that I have overcome, I still feel a sense of unfulfilment within my life which I aim to put right in the coming years. It is just a shame that you as a reader will not be able to chart this success on paper but who knows, there could be scope for a sequel? (But don't hold your breath).

The sense of personal fulfilment or lack of it is not related in any way to the support of key figures in my life. They seem to have generated more ambition and determination for my future career than I do and continue to support and inspire me to embark on a whole host of new projects and challenges. It is more to do with again, my own personal demons which are unable to prevent a comparison between myself and others. I understand that I am different and therefore have a different set of priorities from the average person, but that doesn't stop the mental processes in my mind which lead me to think of myself as a relative failure (is that too strong a word?)

Equally, that does not mean that I am not content with all the things I have done and the people around me who mean a lot. Perhaps the Beatles were right and love is actually all you need.

During my gap year in 2009, whilst waiting to return to Uni to embark on my masters at Bournemouth and with my Gran having just passed away, I started to reflect on my life so far. I created a poem for my upcoming charity show. I was relatively new to the world of poetry and didn't know what I would be like. Let's face it, I am not exactly Pam Ayres, but the following extract is a poem which I think perfectly sums up my relationship with people.

Peoples' Song

We always hope and pray,
All our memories and yesterdays,
Will be able to survive,
Many laughs we shared,
With people who cared,
And cherish every time,
Then music enters our ears,
And reminds us of those many happy years.
People come and people go,
Memories ebb and memories flow,
We couldn't have travelled this road without them,
Find a place, find a time,
To remember those who made life so worthwhile,
But you can't disguise,
The significant people in our lives,
People in our lives.
They pick us up when we are down,
Remind us that we are all clowns,
We laughed out loud,
As we knew someone was proud.
Maybe it was the time we spent,
Maybe it was the messages they sent,
But I will never forget,
People in our lives,
People come and people go,
Memories ebb and memories flow,
We couldn't have travelled this road without them,
Find a place, find a time,
To remember those who made life so worthwhile,
But you can't disguise,
The significant people in our lives,
People in our lives.

This poem epitomises the special relationship which I have been forced to create with people in my time on earth. Throughout my life, despite being a relatively independent person I have always lived through people. Not in the way that I am content in watching others live their lives while I am just merely an observer, but I love being with people and nothing gives me greater pleasure than forming bonds with those that I deem to possess a lot in common with. This side of my life I like to think of as a piece of art, colourful with endless textures and whenever you look at it you always see something different. My Gran was a great ambassador for this idea, as no matter what was happening in her life and the problems she had to overcome the grass was still green and the flowers were always in bloom. It is always these types of people in your life who will get you through the toughest of times and I am lucky enough to have some of the cream of the crop.

At the end of every book the reader is excused for reflecting if indeed it was a good buy (or if it was a present you have my sincere apologies). It is very clear I have not become the first black president of America or sailed single-handed around the world, or even seen my name in lights, but I really hope you appreciate that this is a human story. Not of bravery or heroic acts of courage and selflessness but a man attempting to simply get on with life in the acknowledgement of the barriers he faces. Whatever you do, don't leave this book feeling sorry for me or my situation, as this is not what this book has been about. Just remember it is evidence that life does go on and it is possible to live an ordinary life with many challenges facing you each day.

I am proud that my life is the life which I have carefully chosen and mastered for myself. I have the drive and the determination to overcome the barriers facing me. It is also a testament to all around me. Who else can say their life is about teamwork (well except Pinocchio!) and the cohesion of different characters working together for their benefit? I have been so lucky that all members of this special, unique team have the same ethic of improving the quality of my life and, sorry to use a cliché, but they have made the impossible seem not only possible but the norm. I am extremely grateful that I have been given the opportunity to make such a large group of fantastic friends. So as this is coming towards its climax, as another old cliché goes, I could not have embarked on a project of this magnitude without the support of those friends, both past and present, along with my family, who have made me who I am and made what I can achieve today a possibility, (not just in the writing of this book). Also to the people who inspired me to take an interest in writing at an early age, the people who showed me that I could live an independent lifestyle and beyond all else, to the people who made me feel like I was just a normal guy who had the world at his feet.

So as a reader if you are still wondering why a disabled thirty-year old man finds it relevant to write an autobiography at such a tender age, then maybe this was not the book for you and I can only apologise. Yet if you are still intrigued as to the development of my mainstream life, perhaps you feel a little cheated as well. It is very clear that my life is not a mainstream life at all, nor is it a bad life, but it is, as the title suggests, an adapted life and for that I am very proud.

Beyond The Title

If you would like to hear some of our interviews or find out more about my company, please go to:

http://www.beyondthetitle.co.uk/

You can also follow me on Facebook:

https://www.facebook.com/beyondthetitle

Josh

FCM Publishing

For Creative Minds

I sincerely hope you enjoyed this book.

If you'd like to know more about our forthcoming titles, authors and special events, or to be notified of early releases then email us at:

follow@fcmmedia.co.uk

or come find us on the web at:

www.fcmpublishing.co.uk

or on Twitter at:

@fcmtaryn

We love what we do and we'd like you to be part of a thriving community of people who enjoy books and the very best reading experiences.

Taryn

Taryn Johnston
Creative Director
FCM Media Group